Ebo Botchway

Willingness To Pay For Improved Urban Water Supply

Ebo Botchway

Willingness To Pay For Improved Urban Water Supply

LAP LAMBERT Academic Publishing

Impressum / Imprint
Bibliografische Information der Deutschen Nationalbibliothek: Die Deutsche Nationalbibliothek verzeichnet diese Publikation in der Deutschen Nationalbibliografie; detaillierte bibliografische Daten sind im Internet über http://dnb.d-nb.de abrufbar.
Alle in diesem Buch genannten Marken und Produktnamen unterliegen warenzeichen-, marken- oder patentrechtlichem Schutz bzw. sind Warenzeichen oder eingetragene Warenzeichen der jeweiligen Inhaber. Die Wiedergabe von Marken, Produktnamen, Gebrauchsnamen, Handelsnamen, Warenbezeichnungen u.s.w. in diesem Werk berechtigt auch ohne besondere Kennzeichnung nicht zu der Annahme, dass solche Namen im Sinne der Warenzeichen- und Markenschutzgesetzgebung als frei zu betrachten wären und daher von jedermann benutzt werden dürften.

Bibliographic information published by the Deutsche Nationalbibliothek: The Deutsche Nationalbibliothek lists this publication in the Deutsche Nationalbibliografie; detailed bibliographic data are available in the Internet at http://dnb.d-nb.de.
Any brand names and product names mentioned in this book are subject to trademark, brand or patent protection and are trademarks or registered trademarks of their respective holders. The use of brand names, product names, common names, trade names, product descriptions etc. even without a particular marking in this works is in no way to be construed to mean that such names may be regarded as unrestricted in respect of trademark and brand protection legislation and could thus be used by anyone.

Coverbild / Cover image: www.ingimage.com

Verlag / Publisher:
LAP LAMBERT Academic Publishing
ist ein Imprint der / is a trademark of
AV Akademikerverlag GmbH & Co. KG
Heinrich-Böcking-Str. 6-8, 66121 Saarbrücken, Deutschland / Germany
Email: info@lap-publishing.com

Herstellung: siehe letzte Seite /
Printed at: see last page
ISBN: 978-3-659-31152-9

Copyright © 2013 AV Akademikerverlag GmbH & Co. KG
Alle Rechte vorbehalten. / All rights reserved. Saarbrücken 2013

DEDICATION

Great is thy faithfulness, oh Lord! This work is dedicated to God Almighty, maker of Heaven and Earth. I also dedicate this work to my entire family and all my friends.

ACKNOWLEDGEMENT

Glory be to God Almighty for my life and His immense protection and support especially during this research. Lord, where would I have been had it not been you on my side? Life would have been so meaningless had it not been the abundant grace and tender mercies of the Almighty God.

My indebtedness cannot be measured when it comes to thinking of the efforts of people whose contributions in diverse ways have made this work a success. I acknowledge with much appreciation the support of Dr. D. K. Twerefou and Dr. K. A. Tutu all of the Department of Economics, University of Ghana, for their fruitful suggestions, valuable guidance and words of encouragement. I am also appreciative to Dr. D. K. Twerefou for the financial support provided to enable me undertake the field survey.

I am also grateful to all the lectures and staff of the Department of Economics for their various suggestions and help in one way or another for the production of this work. The African Economic Research Consortium (AERC) cannot be left out in the efforts they made to make this work a success and to all my colleagues, I thank you for your various constructive criticisms and the needed suggestions that made this work a success.

I am heavily indebted to my father Mr. Robert Kwamina Botchway, my mother Madam Agnes Quainoo and my siblings Benjamin Stephen Sarkodie, Kwesi Botchway, Mary B. Botchway, Kwadwo B. Botchway, Mary Botchway, Grace Acquah, Kwasi Botchway and Kwame Odame Botchway for their tremendous assistance in all feasible ways throughout my university education.

My sincere appreciation also goes to Mr. Alfred Opoku Adom, Mr. Benjamin Kwaku Asante, Mr. Owusu-Agyemang Dacosta, Mr. Bernard Antwi, Mr. Isaac Kweku Quainoo, Mr. Ernest Tannor, Madam Rebecca Mensah, Madam Constance Antwi, Mr. Asante Antwi, Ms. Gifty Arthur, Ms. Edna Serwaa Oteng, Ms. Abiba Bala, Ms. Ernestina Obeng, Ms. Gloria Esme Prah Gaisie, Mr. Samuel Appiah Antwi, Mr. Prince Akwasi Antwi, and Ms. Millicent Serwaa Frimpong for their tireless support and prayers for the success of this research. To all my friends not mentioned here, you are not forgotten for you contributed in diverse ways towards the success of this research, may the good Lord bless you all. Amen.

TABLE OF CONTENTS

DEDICATION i
ACKNOWLEDGEMENT ii
TABLE OF CONTENTS iii
LIST OF FIGURES vi
LIST OF TABLES vii
LIST OF ABBREVIATIONS viii
CHAPTER ONE 1
INTRODUCTION 1
  1.1   Background 1
  1.2   Problem Statement 3
  1.3   Objective of the Study 5
  1.4   Significance of the Study 5
  1.5   Organisation of the Study 5
  1.6   Limitation of Study 5
CHAPTER TWO 7
OVERVIEW OF POTABLE WATER DEMAND AND SUPPLY IN ACCRA-TEMA METROPOLIS 7
  2.1   Water Supply in Accra-Tema metropolis 8
  2.3   Demand for Water 11
  2.3   Cost of Water 13
CHAPTER THREE 16
LITERATURE REVIEW 16
  3.1   Theoretical Literature 16
      3.1.1   Economic Valuation of Environmental Resources 16
      3.1.2   Valuation Methods 18
          3.1.2.1   Revealed Willingness to Pay 18
              3.1.2.1.1   Travel Cost Method (TCM) 19
              3.1.2.1.2   Random Utility Modelling (RUM) 20
              3.1.2.1.3   Averting Behaviour Model (ABM) 21
              3.1.2.1.4   Hedonic Pricing Method (HPM) 22

  3.1.2.1.5 Market Price Method (MPM) 24
  3.1.2.1.6 Production Factor Method (PFM) 24
 3.1.2.2 Imputed Willingness to Pay Methods 26
 3.1.2.3 Express Preference/Express Willingness to Pay Method 27
  3.1.2.3.1 Contingent Valuation Method (CVM) 28
  3.1.2.3.2 Willingness to Pay (WTP) versus Willingness to Accept (WTA) 31
  3.1.2.3.3 Choice Experiment Method (CEM) 32
3.2 Empirical Literature Review 33
 3.2.1 Willingness to pay: Improved Water Services 33
 3.2.2 WTP on Other Related Resources 37

CHAPTER FOUR 40
METHODOLOGY 40
4.1 Survey Instrument 40
4.2 Pilot Survey, Pretesting and Training 40
4.3 Sample Frame 41
4.4 Design Survey Questionnaire and Elicitation Format 41
4.5 Field Operations 42
4.6 Data Analysis 42
4.7 Theoretical Framework 43
 4.7.1 The Ordered Probit model 44
4.8 Model Specification 47
 4.8.1 Description of Explanatory Variables 48

CHAPTER FIVE 51
EMPIRICAL RESULTS AND DISCUSSION 51
5.1 Descriptive Analysis 51
 5.1.1 Socioeconomic Characteristics of the Surveyed Households 51
 5.1.2 Respondents Ranking of Social Services 53
 5.1.3 Existing/Current Water Use Conditions and Problems 54
 5.1.4 Existing Household Sanitation Practice 56
 5.1.5 WTP and Starting Bids 57
5.2 Estimated Ordered Probit Model 57

5.3	Total Willingness to Pay and Total Revenue	62

CHAPTER SIX 69

CONCLUSION AND RECOMMENDATIONS 69

    6.1   Conclusion 69

    6.2   Recommendations 70

REFERENCES 72

Appendix A: Correlation Matrix for Explanatory Variables 80

Appendix B: Test for Goodness of fit 81

Appendix C: Econometric estimation of WTP for improved water supply system 82

Appendix D: Estimated marginal effects of the Ordered Probit Model 83

Appendix E: Estimation of the Demand Equation 85

Appendix F: Estimation of Various Consumer Surpluses and Expected Total Revenue Using different tariff levels (Current tariff level of GHp1.45, half of the mean WTP which equals GHp5 and the mean WTP of GHp10) 87

Appendix G: Contingent Valuation Survey Questionnaire 93

Appendix H: How Sachet water producers stores their raw material (water) using water produced by the GWCL. 97

Appendix I: An example of burst pipe resulting in UfW 98

LIST OF FIGURES

Page

Figure 2.1: Water Supply and UfW in Accra-Tema metropolis 2008-2010 16

Figure 2.2: Customer Metering 2008-2010 18

Figure 2.3: Demand and Supply of water in Ghana 22

Figure 5.1: Respondents Level of Education..……...96

Figure 5.2: Age Distribution of Respondents ……………………………………....97

Figure 5.3: Respondents ranking of Social Services ……………………………….99

Figure 5.4: Household's Demand for Water ……………………………………….120

Figure 5.5: Current revenue and consumers' surplus from charging the current price..122

Figure 5.6: Expected Revenue and consumers' surplus from charging half of mean WTP..123

Figure 5.7: Expected Revenue and consumers' surplus from charging the Mean WTP..124

Figure A.1: Expected revenue and consumers' surplus from charging the current tariff..147

Figure A.2: Expected Revenue and consumers' surplus from charging half of the mean WTP..151

Figure A.3: Expected Revenue and consumers' surplus from charging the mean WTP..153

Figure A4: Polytanks containing water to be used for sachet water production......161

Figure A5: A picture of a pipe spilling over…………………………………….....162

LIST OF TABLES

Page

Table 2.1: Selected year's tariffs approved by the PURC since its inception in 1997....26

Table 4.1: Deterministic Statistics of the Explanatory Variables 93

Table 5.1: Households Major source of water 100

Table 5.2: Number of Days that water flows in a Week 101

Table 5.3: Number of Hours that Water Flows in a Day 102

Table 5.4: Existing Household Sanitation Practice 104

Table 5.5: Ordered Probit estimate of determinants of WTP for improved water supply services..107

Table 5.6: Estimated marginal effects of the Ordered Probit Model 113

Table 5.7: Analysis of Maximum WTP reported from the open ended question.........116

Table 5.8: Total WTP and Total Revenue for Improved Water Service (pesewas per bucket)..118

LIST OF ABBREVIATIONS

ABM   Averting Behaviour Method
ARUM   Additive Random Utility Model
CEM   Choice Experiment Method
CV   Compensating Variation
CVM   Contingent Valuation Method
CWSA   Community Water and Sanitation Agency
CWSD   Community Water and Sanitation Division
DCM   Damage Cost Model
DUV   Direct Use Value
EV   Equivalent Variation
GHp   Ghana pesewas
GWCL   Ghana Water Company Limited
GWSC   Ghana Water and Sewerage Corporation
HPM   Hedonic Price Model
IFPRI   International Food Policy Research Institute
IIA   Independence of Irrelevant Alternatives
IUV   Indirect Use Value
LR(I)   Likelihood Ratio (Index)
MDG(s)   Millennium Development Goal(s)
MPM   Market Price Model
NUV   Non-Use Value
OLS   Ordinary Least Squares
PFM   Production Function Method
PURC   Public Utilities Regulatory Commission
RCM   Replacement Cost model
RUM   Random Utility Model

SCM	Substitute Cost Model
TCM	Travel Cost Model
TEV	Total Economic Value
UfW	Unaccounted for Water
UNICEF	United Nations Children's Fund
WHO	World Health Organisation
WTA	Willingness to Accept
WTP	Willingness to Pay

CHAPTER ONE

INTRODUCTION

1.1 Background

Clean and safe drinking water is a basic human need. "All people, whatever their stage of development and socioeconomic status have the right to have access to drinking water in quantities and of a quality equal to their basic needs" (UN, 1977). Water is the most important necessity to life after oxygen. Thus, anything that inhibits the provision and supply of water tends to affect the very existence of humanity. It is also said that water is life, and just as everyone has the right to life, access to potable and safe drinking water makes it a basic human right. According to medical experts, water takes a greater portion of the human body and its presence alone helps keep the human body in great shape. In this context, it has been advised that, it is good for every human being to take at least 2 litres of water a day[1].

Most of the challenges facing many developing countries in the world today in their struggle for economic and social development are increasingly related to water. Water as well as oxygen is the most valuable natural resource, vital for the existence of any form of life and for achieving sustainable development. Poverty assessment research has consistently shown that improvement in water supply services is a critical element in designing and implementing effective strategies for poverty alleviation. Topfer (1998) argues that an adequate supply of safe and clean water is the most important precondition for sustaining human life, for maintaining ecosystems that support all life and for achieving sustainable development. Therefore, recent renewed focus on poverty alleviation and good health has resulted in increased attention to the benefits of improved water accessibility.

In view of this, improving the adequacy and quality of water supplies is a priority for the United Nations. In an attempt by the United Nations to alleviate poverty, one of the goals set for the year 2015 in the United Nations Millennium Declaration and in the Plan of Implementation of the World Summit on Sustainable Development is to reduce the population without adequate access to water and basic sanitation by half (UN, 2006).

According to the United Nations (2002) about 1.1 billion people representing 18% of the world's population lack access to safe drinking water. Whereas access to sufficient and clean drinking water is not a problem for the developed world, more than 5 million people perish every year from water-related diseases in the developing world largely as a result of poor access to clean water.

Africa has the lowest water supply coverage among all the regions in the world. The World Health Organization (WHO) in the year 2000 estimated that Africa has 28% of the world's population without access to potable water supply and only 62% of the people in African countries have access to potable water. It is also estimated that 30% of Africans residing in the urban areas currently lack access to adequate water services and facilities.

---

[1] http://news.peacefmonline.com/features/201001/36040.php

It is therefore estimated that, urban Africa requires about 6000 to 8000 new connections of water supply every day in order to meet the recently established MDGs of halving the population without access to potable water by 2015.

Shortcomings in the water supply service in large urban areas of developing countries are a critical problem affecting millions of people (New Delhi Declaration, 1990; Dublin, 1992; WHO and UNICEF, 2000). According to the United Nations (1995), almost half of the world's population live in urban areas and most population growth are taking place in the developing world. Thus, the enormous volumes of water and the cost of extensive infrastructure required to fulfil urban water demand have frequently exceeded the ability of government to provide secure supplies (Munasinghe, 1990; Hardoy et al., 1992; Serageldin, 1994; Drakakis-Smith, 2000). This has resulted in a situation where a large proportion of the human population resorts to the use of potentially harmful sources of water.

The implication of this collective failure has resulted in billions of people locked in a cycle of poverty and disease. Inadequate provisions of water and sanitation are the main causes of diseases that arise from contaminated food and water which are among the world's leading causes of premature death and serious illness. The World Health Organization (WHO) and United Nations Children's Fund (UNICEF) estimated in 2004 that, about 2.2 million people are killed by diarrhoea (which results from poor water quality) every year and that about 1.8 million are from developing countries. Brown (2003) also argues that many people in the world's hospitals today are suffering from water related diseases than any ailment. Further records show that about 2 million children every year, which is about 6000 a day, die from such infections, out of which 1.6 million are from the developing world (UNICEF, 2003).

In Ghana, diarrhoea accounts for 12% of childhood deaths and it is the third largest cause of death for children under the age of 5 after malaria and pneumonia (WHO, 2006). Also 61 people had died from cholera in Ghana in 2011. According to Dowdeswell (1996), about 80% of all diseases and more than one third of all deaths in developing countries are caused by contaminated water and poor sanitation. United Nations (2002) confirmed that with adequate supplies of potable drinking water, incidence of some illness and for that matter death could drop by as much as 75%. Emphasizing on the importance of water Nielsen (2004) argues that safe drinking water is not just a luxury. It often makes the difference between life and death.

Rainfall in Ghana is not scarce and several rivers do not cease to flow, but potable water is denied millions of people. Similar to the urban water sector in many developing countries, there are serious constraints to meeting the challenge to provide potable water for all urban residents. Water supply shortages and quality deterioration are among the problems which require greater attention and action. Various strategies have been developed to make potable water accessible to all inhabitants but the situation has not significantly improved.

1.2 Problem Statement

Many developing countries have often subsidised potable water supply, typically in an attempt to achieve social and health benefits for low-income households forming the large majority of the urban population. However, benefits of subsidised water accrue primarily to the wealthier households whereas poorer households benefit in a less than proportionate manner due to poor targeting of subsidies. According to the Public Utilities Regulatory Commission (PURC) of Ghana, majority of urban households depend on secondary water providers like tankers, cart operators and domestic vendors, at a cost that is 12 times[2] more than the approved price. When this happens, the drain on government revenues represented by the subsidy can hamper its ability to expand and improve the service provided to the urban poor.

In Ghana, water tariffs are too low to recover the costs of the service[3]. Water tariffs in rural areas tend to be higher than in urban areas. The average water tariff in Ghana's urban areas between 1990 and 1997 ranged from GH¢0.02 to GH¢0.03 per cubic meter. During this period, the Government was not willing to approve major tariff increases. However, with the establishment of the PURC which autonomously examines and approve public service tariff, there have been significant improvements in water tariffs although they remain below recovery levels. In 2004, average water tariff was GH¢0.45 per cubic meter (WaterAid, 2005). In 2006, GWCL's tariff for the first 20m³ consumed was GH¢0.50 per m³, whereas GH¢0.70 was charged for each cubic metre exceeding 20m³ within a month (Doe, 2007). Currently, domestic consumers are paying a rate of GH¢0.80 per cubic metre for the first 20m³ consumed in a month. A rate of GH¢1.20 is charged per any additional cubic metre consumed above the life line of 20m³ consumption in a month.

Even though the MDGs target is to half the population without potable water supply and sanitation by 2015, Ghana aims to achieve 85% coverage of both water supply and sanitation by 2015 which is a higher coverage ratio than MDGs target. According to WaterAid's calculations, the expansion and rehabilitation of urban infrastructure to meet MDGs targets requires investment of US$85 million a year, but the current level of investment is estimated to be US$17 million. This implies that about US$68 million worth of investment in the water sector is required to achieve the MDGs target[4].

From the population and housing census[5] of 2010, the population of the Accra-Tema metropolis stood at 4,192,370 with Accra's population alone being 3,963,264. Statistics show that about 80% of households in Accra and Tema have access to potable drinking water. This does not imply that all houses get their source of water from the GWCL which is charged with the responsibility of providing potable water. In reality only 45% of the population have a household connection or at best a yard connection (Abraham et. al, 2007).

---

[2] http://www.switchurbanwater.eu/outputs/pdfs/W6-2_CACC_POS_demo_A1.pdf

[3] http://en.wikipedia.org/wiki/Water_supply_and_sanitation_in_Ghana
[4] http://en.wikipedia.org/wiki/Water_supply_and_sanitation_in_Ghana
[5] http://en.wikipedia.org/wiki/Ghana

A major problem that confronts residents is the quality and quantity of water supplied. The current water production in the Accra-Tema metropolis is about 394,260m^3 per day. With GWCL's unaccounted for water (UfW) at about 60% of total output, the volume of water that is effectively sold per day is approximately 158,000m^3 (GWCL, 2010) which is less than a quarter of daily demand.[6] Even though it is conceived that a fair percentage of UfW is also used by urban residents, there still remains an acute shortage of water as demonstrated by a widespread rationing in the metropolis.

According to estimates by WaterAid (2005) only a quarter of the residents in Accra and Tema receive a continuous supply of water, about 30% are provided with water for 12 hours each day, five days a week. Another 35% are supplied for 2 days each week. The remaining population who live mainly on the outskirts of these cities are completely without access to potable water.

Added to this problem is the quality of the water supplied. Good quality water is defined by the World Health Organization (WHO) as *"water which is suitable for human consumption and for all normal domestic purposes, including personal hygiene"*. This definition implies that the use of water should not present any kind of health risk such as chemical irritation, intoxication or microbiological infection harmful to human health. Labite et al. (2008) assessment of the water supply system in Ghana concluded that, the failure in the treatment or distribution process has affected the quality of drinking water in Ghana. It is estimated that, if the population of Accra continues to grow at its current growth rate (3.36%), then the population will increase by about 5 million in the year 2030. This will further put pressure on the existing supply. As the population increases, demand for water also increases and thus if the current water resources are not properly utilized, the water supply system will collapse (Awuah and Assan, 2007).

The continuous public outcry about the quantity and quality of water provision in the metropolis is a clear indication of households' desire for clean uninterrupted water supply. Also, poor households paying 12 times the approved water tariff for inadequate water suggest that they will be willing to pay for improved water supply systems. Currently, many international financing agencies contend that the necessary resources needed for the provision of improved water supply need to come from domestic consumers (World Bank, 1991; Brookshire and Whittington, 1993). Juxtaposing this demand to the claim by the GCWL that their inability to meet this demand is mainly due to financial constraints[7] indicates that supply can improve if households are willing and able to pay for good quality water. Research questions that confront the metropolis today are: How much are households willing to pay for improved water services? What factors influence the Willingness to pay (WTP) for improved water services? What is the cost of inadequate and poor quality water supply? At what tariff level will the maximum revenue be obtained?

---

[6] In 2005, the daily demand of water in the metropolis as reported by WaterAid was about 763,300m^3.

[7] The GCWL reported in 2009 that the company the company need about US$ 68 million capital investment to give a new and improved water production system to be able to meet government's 85% coverage target of 2015.

1.3 Objective of the Study

The overall objective of the study is to assess the WTP for improved water supply and the factors that influence the WTP. Specifically the study seeks to determine the:

1. WTP for improved water supply in the Accra-Tema metropolis.
2. Tariff level that maximizes revenue.
3. Economic cost of inadequate and poor quality water supply.
4. Factors that affect the WTP for improved water supply.

1.4 Significance of the Study

In Ghana, water provision facilities have invariably fallen into disuse because the approach used to run them has failed to ensure sustainability of the service. Various strategies are always being developed to make water accessible to all inhabitants, but due to insufficient funds and structures, the gap between demand and supply of water continues to widen. This study is important because it will help policy makers to have a good idea of how much households are prepared to pay for improved water supply system with the view of solving the current water crises in the metropolis.

A similar work was done by Adjei (1999) but this work uses data from 1991 and only estimates the willingness to pay by households for improved water supply services in the metropolis. This study will go further by estimating the demand curve for improved urban water supply in the metropolis and also determine the tariff level that will maximise total revenue. The study will also provide policy makers the value of the cost of inadequate and poor quality water supplied to households. In a nut shell, it will help policy makers to identify the factors influencing the WTP for improved water supply system and thereby providing a framework for developing a comprehensive tariff system for urban areas in the country.

1.5 Organisation of the Study

The study comprises of six (6) chapters. The first chapter looks at the general background of the study, the statement of the problem, the objectives of the study and the significance of the study. The second chapter take a look at the supply of water, the demand for water and the cost of water in the Accra-Tema metropolis. Available data on the demand and supply are briefly surveyed. Chapter three contains a review of both theoretical and empirical work on environmental resources. The main focus in this chapter is on willingness to pay using contingent valuation method with special reference to water, though other resources are considered briefly. The fourth chapter explains the methodology adopted by the study. The fifth chapter talks about the descriptive and empirical analysis of the results and the last chapter concludes the work and looks at the policy recommendations based on the results. This chapter also makes possible suggestion for future research.

1.6 Limitation of Study

The study was done using one of the most popular methods of economic valuation in developed countries which is the Contingent Valuation Method. There are many biases and constraints involved in its application but it is a step toward valuation of environmental quality and it will allow for making decisions of investment with more or better information in cities in developing countries like Accra and Tema.

Furthermore, due to financial constraints and time constraints that precluded the possibility of a more rigorous approach to data collection, the sample survey carried out for the study is limited both in coverage and in size. The sample size was limited to 315 households in the Accra-Tema metropolis. In light of this, data generated for the study should be used with care.

CHAPTER TWO

OVERVIEW OF POTABLE WATER DEMAND AND SUPPLY IN ACCRA-TEMA METROPOLIS

The challenge of water supply in Ghana is an age long phenomenon. Before colonial rule in 1844, each public and private entity; individuals, trading, mining and timber companies and small communities were responsible for developing and managing their water source and supply. In the early 1900s, drought, population growth, gradual migration into more urban areas and health problems from contamination of surface waters led the colonial British government to claim responsibility of public water supply in urban and rural areas. Under British rule, the Public Works Department was created to assess urban water supply and in 1920, the Geological Survey Division was formed to train local authorities in digging wells, protecting the wells with linings, and preventing the contamination of water supplies (Limantol, 2009).

The Ghana Water and Sewerage Corporation (GWSC) was established in 1965 and by a legal Act (310) mandated with the responsibility for the provision, distribution, conservation and management of water supply development and installation, and for the coordination of all activities related to the supply (Gyau-Boakye, 2001). The GWSC as a statutory corporation, remained in operation from 1966 until 1st July, 1999 when it was converted into a Limited Liability Company known as Ghana Water Company Limited (GWCL).

To address the problems that confronted the Ghana water sector, the government in 1993 took a decision to restructure the sector and hence various reforms have been adopted since 1993. The main aims of the reforms were to separate rural and urban water supply services, to introduce independent regulatory agency as well as to include private sector participation (CWSA, 2004).

In line with the reforms, the Community Water and Sanitation Division (CWSD) was established in 1994 as a semi-autonomous division of the GWSC to be responsible for facilitating the community water supply management. In 1999, the GWSC was replaced by the publicly owned Ghana Water Company Limited (GWCL) which was charged with the responsibility of supplying water to urban dwellers. The CWSD was transformed into Community Water and Sanitation Agency (CWSA) to take care of rural water supplies and sanitation. The responsibility of rural water supply and sanitation was then decentralized to the District Assemblies which receive support from the CWSA (WaterAid, 2005).

The other development has been the shift of the regulations of water supply from the government to an independent agency known as the Public Utilities and Regulatory Commission (PURC). The Commission is mandated to be responsible for formulating as well as approving appropriate pricing mechanisms aimed at full cost recovery as subsidization of water services was being faced out by the government in 2003 (OECD, 2007). The Commission regulates only the services of GWCL and for that matter has no hand in the services of community managed systems.

2.1 Water Supply in Accra-Tema metropolis

Water supply for the Accra-Tema metropolis is undertaken by the Ghana Water Company Limited (GWCL) which supplies water from two sources, the Weija Waterworks and the Kpong Water Waterworks. Even though the GWCL supplies water from two sources, it supplies the minimum amount of water to the metropolis. This brings into focus the factors that determine the supply of water in general.

According to the WHO (1984), one of the factors that determine the supply of water to an area is seasonality. World Health Organization argues that, availability of water at the source means a continuous supply of water all things being equal. On the other hand, it is argued that if the volume of water at the source of water supply is unreliable it affects the overall supply of water. A typical example is that, during the dry season, water supply to most towns becomes irregular as a result of dried up rivers and falls in volume of lakes leading to acute water supply shortages. In the Accra-Tema metropolis, there is frequent fall in the volume of water at the sources of supply during the dry seasons thereby leading to acute water supply shortages in the metropolis.

Furthermore, the quality of water at the source also affects the supply of water. It is argued that, high quality water at the source means quick supply since there will be relatively less treatment time. On the other hand, there will be more treatment time for a source that has low quality thereby leading to less frequent supply. In the Accra-Tema metropolis the Weija Lake which is one of the sources of water supplied to the metropolis has had issues of bad quality in recent times as a result of pollution by residents living along the lake and fishing activities by fishermen. This has resulted in more treatment time and thereby contributing to the acute water shortage in the metropolis.

The cost of water supply system is also a core factor that determines the supply of water in an area. Since water tariffs are determined by the PURC and these tariffs are below the cost recovery levels, higher cost on the present system may reduce supply and thereby resulting in irregularity in the provision of the service.

One other factor that determines the supply of water is the distance from the water supply source to consumers. Longer distances may lead to more leakages and burst pipes along the transmission lines. These leakages and burst pipes (which are mostly as a result old and obsolete pipes laid decades ago) contribute a lot to acute water supply shortages.

Another factor that determines the supply of water is the way by which consumers get water. Consumers with household connections will have more regular flow than those who get water from tankers, cart operators and water vendors all things being equal. In the case of stand pipes, people will sometimes have to be in a queue for so long with other users whilst vendor services may be unreliable. The current delivery of water to the Accra-Tema metropolis by GWCL is presented as Figure 2.1.

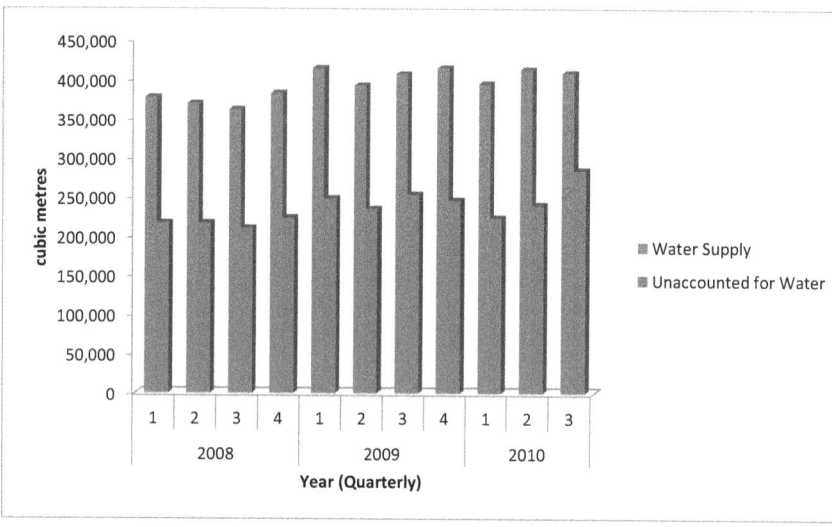

Source: GWCL, 2010.

Figure 2.1: Water Supply and UfW in Accra-Tema metropolis 2008-2010.

The current effective water supply to the Accra-Tema metropolis is about 158,000m^3 per day. This supply does not meet the average daily demand[8] of water in the Accra-Tema metropolis. This problem of inadequate supply of potable drinking water in the Accra-Tema metropolis is enormous. It involves many different aspects of legal, institutional framework, inadequate resources and the lack of interest by stakeholders. According to WaterAid (2005), the inability of the GWCL to solve this acute water shortage in the metropolis is as a result of the dire and worsening financial condition of the company, insufficient sector investment and weak implementation capacity caused by bad management, staffing problems and low salary levels.

One other factor that has contributed immensely to the shortage of water supply in the metropolis is the rate of unaccounted for water. Unaccounted for water (UfW) is a situation where treated water is unaccounted for by the system in that, its precise destination is not known. As shown from Figure 2.1, UfW is estimated at about 60% of average daily production. It continues to be a chronic problem facing the GWCL and has contributed immensely to the GWCL inability to recover cost of supply.

One of the factors that contribute to UfW is leakages and burst pipes and this is as a result of old pipes and gross inefficiency on the part of the GWCL. Most of the time even when distress calls are made to the office of the GWCL as a result of leakages and burst pipes, it takes days for them to respond (see Appendix I).

---

[8] In 2005, the daily demand of water in the metropolis as reported by WaterAid was about 763,300m^3.

Another factor that contributes to UfW is that, several commercial users such as cart operators and vendors are designated as domestic users with uniform rates. These commercial users buy the water at domestic rates and sell them to domestic consumers at a very high price and thereby making supernormal profits. This gives them the incentive to store more of the water and thereby also contributing to the acute water shortage in the metropolis. Furthermore, people divert water from the transmission pipe for agricultural purposes and hence reducing the supply of water to consumers in the metropolis.

Illegal connections that are rampant in the metropolis are another form of UfW. From figure 2.2, it is clear that the GWCL will find it difficult to tell how much water is consumed by households since consumers who do not have effective metres which are as a result of illegal connections account for about 50% of total consumers (GWCL, 2010). According to the GWCL, about 28% of its customers are not billed by the company as indicated by Figure 2.2, and they claim that this is as a result of illegal connections and insufficient personnel. Thus the amount of water consumed by illegally connected customers is unknown and this contributes immensely to UfW.

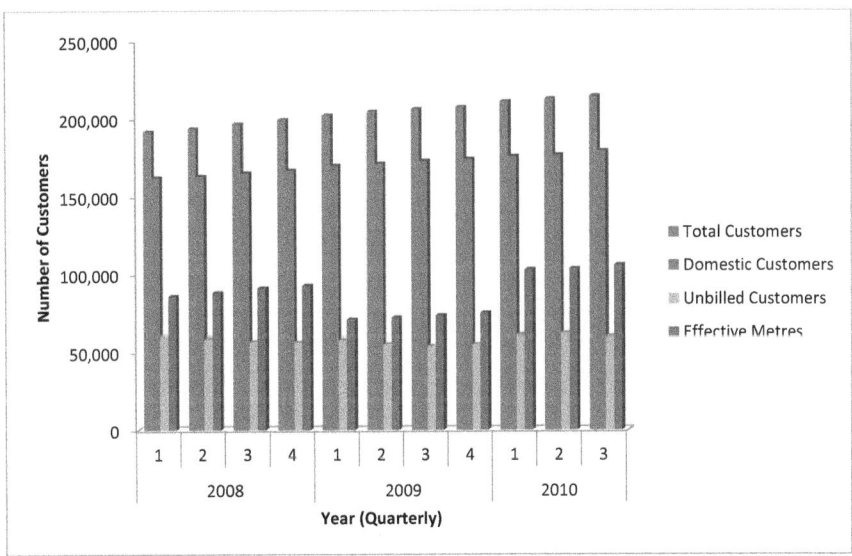

Source: GWCL, 2010.

Figure 2.2: Customer Metering, 2008-2010.

According to the GWCL, one other reason why the Accra-Tema metropolis continues to experience acute water shortage is due to the operations of sachet/bottle mineral water operators. The GWCL argues that, of the amount of water that they produce for consumers in the metropolis, sachet/bottle water producers alone export close to 20% outside to neighbouring Togo, Benin and Cote d'Ivoire. Besides, they also transport large amount of the water produced for consumers in the metropolis to regions such as Ashanti, Western, Central and Eastern regions even though these areas have their own treatment plants. These sachet/bottle water producers use treated water produced by GWCL, meant for consumers in the Accra-Tema metropolis to produce their sachet/bottle water and even store large quantities of them while homes go in search of water for their domestic activities. These activities by sachet/bottle water producers it is argued by the GWCL make it impossible for them to meet the growing water demand in the metropolis[9].

2.3 Demand for Water

Household demand for water is modelled as a final good for consumption similar to that of any other good. The decision to consume more or less is based on a variety of factors including price, weather, income etc.

One factor that influences the demand for water is the climate or weather conditions and cultural patterns in terms of bathing, laundering, cooking and using water for performing other household chores. Global climate change may affect water use in the sense that hotter climates usually demand more water in terms of bathing and washing than cooler climates. The provision of public bathing and laundering facilities in some communities may also increase demand considerably.

Water demanded for productive purposes such as livestock rearing, irrigation of farmlands, preparation of produce for market, processing plants and in some cases the establishment of industries is another type of demand for water. Water used for economic activities increase the demand for water. Changes in the economic base of the community may also have an impact on water demand. Some industries such as bottling plants, pulp and paper plants or breweries tend to have larger water demands, while service industries such as banking and retail generally have smaller demands. In Ghana, the service industry is growing faster than the other sectors of the economy but with increase in sachet/bottle water producers and brewery companies in the Accra-Tema metropolis, there is a larger demand for water in the metropolis.

The growth of the population is also one of the factors that influence water demand. The population of the Accra-Tema metropolis is increasing rapidly and thus, it is estimated that the current water supply system will collapse if the current water resources are not properly utilized (Awuah and Assan, 2007). This is so because as the population increases, demand for water also increases and with little effort made by the stakeholders to improve the water supply system, the system will collapse eventually.

Another factor that influences the demand for water is the housing stock. The age of the housing stock will determine the number of inefficient water using fixtures, particularly toilets. Single detached residences generally have yards. The sector will use more water per household for landscape irrigation than multi-unit housing. Hence, the proportion of single family to multi-unit households will impact water use in the area.

---

[9] http://www.ghananewsagency.org/s_social/r_12236/?utm_source=modrnghanaweb.com&utm_medium=web&utm_campaign=AFL_TrafficShare
(See Appendix H)

The introduction of new technologies is also a factor that influences water demand. New technologies have already resulted in greatly improved efficiencies in toilets, showerheads, clothes washers and there may still be further improvements made in these and other technologies. Other advances such as grey water recycling may eventually be developed to such an extent as to further reduce water demand. This means that improvements in new technology may reduce the demand for water.

In general, it is important to note that, demand for water is highly related to the productive use of water in the house or elsewhere. Water is used as both a good for final consumption as well as an input to various activities such as landscaping, washing clothes, bottling plants and so on. Thus unlike other goods, the determination of water demand differs according to its use or purpose. For example whether the water demanded will be used for domestic purposes, agricultural purposes or for industrial use and so on. In the case of domestic use, a number of special factors such as purity, reliability, quality, quantity and cost among other things are considered.

According to the GWCL, even though water production in Ghana has continued to increase from 201 million cubic metres in 2002 to 232 million cubic metres in 2009, water demand has continuously outstripped water supply. It is estimated that in 2007, water demand was 394 million cubic metres whilst supply was only 218 million cubic metres. In 2008, production increased to 223 million cubic metres and demand increased to 404 million cubic metres, leaving a deficit of 181 million cubic metres. And in 2009, production of water increased further to 232 million cubic metres but demand also rose to 415 million cubic metres leaving a deficit of 185 million cubic metres. As shown in Figure 2.3, even though the supply is increasing over the years, deficit also continues to increase.

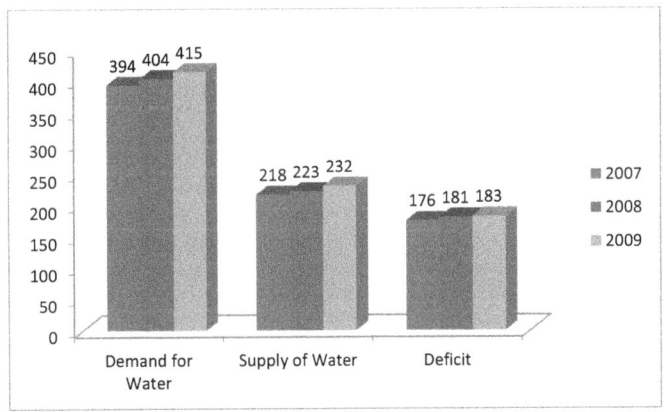

Source: GWCL, 2010.

Figure 2.3: Demand and Supply of water in Ghana.

Water supply interruptions are very much predominant in the metropolis because the demand for water far exceed the supply of water and that is why almost all households have some form of storage facilities in their homes. These forms of storing water will be observed as you move from one household to another in the metropolis. The most common method of storing water among high income households is the use of overhead tanks while middle income households and the urban poor mostly use barrels to store water. In some houses also water is stored in buckets, pots and containers. Water supply interruptions also explain why people are always travelling long distances in search of water. They will have to be in long queues in order to get water from water vendors, cart operators, public standpipes, and sometimes neighbours who have wells or boreholes. People sometimes have to use sachet water for cooking, washing utensils and in extreme cases for bathing.

Nowadays, access to potable water is closely related to wealth. For instance the urban poor in the metropolis gets less water and also pay a higher percentage of their income for water than the middle income and higher income households in the metropolis. This is because most of the urban poor do not have access to piped water and therefore are forced to get water from secondary sources (vendors and cart operators) which are 12 times more expensive than the price GWCL charges. Also, since the urban poor do not have big storage facilities like those of high income, even when the tap is following they cannot store as much water as the rich household will store and therefore resort to the secondary sources again in times of supply interruptions. This clearly indicates that the water supply system in the Accra-Tema metropolis is skewed in favour of the rich and therefore the poor are made to pay more than the rich.

2.3   Cost of Water

Rain water, water from streams, rivers, lakes and the sea are free but there are costs involved in fetching them to ours homes and treat them in order to make it suitable for human consumption. In other words there is an opportunity cost in terms of time involved in travelling long distances in search of water and also treating the water to make it potable. Water from the Weija Lake and Kpong that the GWCL uses is free but there is a cost involved in treating the water in order to make it potable and also transporting to our homes and industries.

Before the introduction of the Economic Recovery Programme (ERP) in 1983 in Ghana, the production of water by the GWSC was highly subsidised (Adjei, 1999). Government support to the GWSC in terms of subsidy ceased a year after the inception of the ERP. Cost recovery measures were introduced which resulted in a regular revision of the water tariffs upwards. During this period, water tariffs were increased between 27% and 168% (Benneh et al, 1993). The rate of the upward revision of water tariffs became a source of worry to consumers over the years. The result of public outcry over the increases in water tariffs resulted in the establishment of the PURC in 1997 which was autonomously charged with the responsibility of examining and approving public service tariff.

The first tariff system approved by the PURC was in March 1998. In that tariff system, domestic consumers were to pay a rate of GH¢0.04 per cubic metre for the first $13m^3$ consumed in a month. Also domestic consumers who consume between 13 and $45m^3$ in a month were to pay a rate of GH¢0.10 per cubic metre and those who consume above

45m³ in a month were to pay a rate of GH¢0.14 per cubic metre. Consumers who were using public standpipes were to pay a rate of GH¢0.025 per each cubic metre consumed.

In 1999, the GWSC proposed an increase of between 76% and 100% in water tariff but only between 20% and 30% increase was approved by the PURC. The schedule of the tariffs approved by the PURC since its inception in 1997 is depicted by Table 2.1.

There was also a slight increase in the price of water in the year 2001 and in 2004; average water tariff for domestic consumers was GH¢0.45 per cubic meter (WaterAid, 2005). In 2006, GWCL's tariff for the first 20m³ consumed was GH¢0.50 per m³, whereas GH¢0.70 was charged for each cubic metre exceeding 20m³ consumed by domestic consumers within a month (Doe, 2007).

Though there have been major increases in the price of water since the inception of the PURC in 1997, they remain far below cost recovery levels. The low level of the price of water is one of the main causes of the poor service provided by the GWCL. In order to encourage the GWCL to provide better and efficient services, prices must be raised so that they will just be equal to cost recovery levels. It is in this regard that some international financing agencies contend that the necessary resources needed for the provision of improved water supply need to come from domestic consumers.

Table 2.1 Selected year's tariffs approved by PURC since its inception in 1997

Year	Category of Service	Monthly Consumption	Approved Rate	
1998	Metered (Domestic)	0-13	GH¢0.04	
		14-45	GH¢0.10	
		above 45	GH¢0.14	
	Commercial/Industrial	0-45	GH¢0.13	
		46-450	GH¢0.16	
		above 450	GH¢0.20	
	Public Standpipes		GH¢0.025	
	Public Institutions/ Government Dept.		GH¢0.12	
	Unmetered Premise (Flat rate per house per month)			GH¢0.52
	Boreholes, Wells, Hand pumps (Flat rate per house per month)			GH¢0.10
1999	Metered (Domestic)	0-10	GH¢0.05	
		11-40	GH¢0.13	
		above 40	GH¢0.182	
	Commercial/Industrial	0-40	GH¢0.182	
		41-450	GH¢0.223	
		above 450	GH¢0.223	
	Public Standpipes		GH¢0.04	
	Public Institutions/ Government Dept.		GH¢0.156	
	Unmetered Premise (Flat rate per house per month)			GH¢0.65
	Boreholes, Wells, Hand pumps (Flat rate per house per month)			GH¢0.15
2001	Metered (Domestic)	0-10	GH¢0.099	
		above 10	GH¢0.36	
	Commercial/Industrial		GH¢0.40	
	Public Standpipes		GH¢0.10	
	Public Institutions/ Government Dept.		GH¢0.36	
	Unmetered Premise (Flat rate per house per month)			GH¢0.99
	Boreholes, Wells, Hand pumps (Flat rate per house per month)			GH¢0.30
2010	Metered (Domestic)	0-20	GH¢0.80	
		Above 21	GH¢1.20	
	Commercial/Industrial (Flat rate)		GH¢1.80	
	Public Standpipes		GH¢0.80	
	Public Institutions / Government Dept.		GH¢1.54	
	Unmetered Premise (Flat rate per house per month)			GH¢5.20

Source: PURC, 2010.

CHAPTER THREE

LITERATURE REVIEW

This chapter explains why no other valuation technique was used but rather the Contingent Valuation Method (CVM) was used in the study. The strengths of the CVM over other valuation techniques have also been discussed briefly. The Chapter also looks at the relationship between willingness to pay (WTP) and willingness to accept (WTA). It also discusses empirical work on improved water supply services and other resources that have been done using the Contingent Valuation Method (CVM) and willingness to pay.

3.1   Theoretical Literature

3.1.1   Economic Valuation of Environmental Resources

Environmental goods and services are the biogeochemical processes, attributes or the products that relate to the self-maintenance of an ecosystem, provision of wildlife habitat, unique landscapes, hydrological services, cultural and rural heritage, cycling of carbon, nitrogen, sulphur, phosphorous, water or trapping of nutrients and open-air recreational opportunities etc. and make the basis for sustenance as well as prosperity to the human society. They are often known as non-market or non-monetary benefits because they are not captured in economic markets and people do not pay money to receive them. Only a few of these environmental goods and services have markets and therefore, prices of only a few are available. These prices available are also only indicators of the minimal payments at which producers and consumers have agreed to enter in transactions. Therefore at these prices there may be substantial producer and/or consumer surpluses that may go unaccounted for. The economic value of environmental goods and services include these unaccounted surpluses, but their low prices do not reflect their worth. Moreover, many environmental goods and services have no markets and therefore have no prices at which they are available to consumers. Economic valuation of such goods and services is much more important to their sustainability (Appau-Danso, 2004).

The main reason why these environmental goods are not marketable is because they have the characteristics of public goods[10]. That is, they are non-rival in consumption. They may be consumed by many without adversely affecting each other's interest. The other characteristic is non-excludability. That is, no-one can be excluded from consuming the good. These two features mean that if all relevant individuals acted to further their own personal interest the goods will be undersupplied, the market would fail and could lead to extinction of the good. Public goods often suffer from free-rider problem. This is because although each user values them, none has an incentive to pay to maintain them.

The theory of economic valuation is based on individual preferences and choices (Perman et al, 2003). The study of this subject is at the centre of modern microeconomic theory and is closely linked with the subject of allocation of scarce environmental resources to alternative ends. Economic value is measured by the maximum someone is willing to

---

[10] http://en.wikipedia.org/wiki/Environmental_good

give up in other goods and services in order to obtain a good, service or a state of the world. The market price of a good or service in most cases does not correctly measure the economic value of that good and service. Many people are actually willing to pay more than the market price for a good and thus their WTP exceeds the market price.

The general economic theory based on the Marshallian approach claims that individuals maximises their utility/satisfaction subject to a budget constraint. The basic flaw of the Marshallian approach is the assumption that nominal income is constant. Under the Hicksian approach, an individual is claimed to minimise his expenditure subject to a constant utility. Under this approach the individual's nominal income is assumed not to be constant. In other words, Hicks-compensated demand functions shows the quantities consumed at various prices assuming that income is adjusted (compensated), so that utility is held constant at a specified utility level. The difference between the Hicks-compensated and the Marshalls-ordinary demand functions is one of the main considerations in the comparison of equivalent variation (EV), compensating variation (CV) and consumer surplus measures of welfare change (Wattage, 2002).

The Total Economic Value (TEV) of a resource such as improved water supply can be broken down into two main categories: Use Value (UV) and Non-Use Value (NUV). In other words TEV = UV + NUV.

Use Value refers to those benefits that originate from society's gains from using, or potentially using a given environmental resource or its services. For instance, individuals use a clean river more effectively for drinking, swimming, boating and washing without paying for these services. Use value includes Direct Use Value (DUV) and Indirect Use Value (IUV). Thus, UV = DUV + IUV.

The Direct Use Value of an asset is the contribution that the assets make to current production or consumption or the value derived from directly consuming services provided by an environmental good. Logging the forest to obtain fuel wood and fishing for subsistence are examples of direct use value. Indirect use value refers to the benefits resulting from the functional services that the environment provides to support current consumption and production (Perman et al., 2003). For example, a forest provides watershed protection and the Ozone layer protects the Earth from ultraviolet radiation.

The Non-Use Value of a resource refers to the value that individuals attach to the resource in appreciation of the resource when they are actually not using the resource. These values are the manifestation of people's willingness to pay for a resource regardless of their ability to make any use of it now, or in the future (Perman et al., 2003). The Non-Use Value consists of Options Value, Existence Value and Bequest Value. That is, NUV = Options Value + Existence Value + Bequest Value.

Option Value is the present willingness to pay based on the future benefit to be derived from an unutilised asset when the option to use it will be excised. In other words, an environmental good will have an option value if the future benefits it might yield are uncertain and the depletion of the resource is effectively irreversible. In this case, one will be willing to pay merely to preserve the resource simply because it might prove valuable at some time in the future. The value of options is derived from the fact that present time information is not perfect (Perman et al., 2003).

Existence Value refers to the satisfaction of merely knowing that the asset exists, although the person assigning the value has no intention of using it. It is the utility derived from the existence of an environmental good. That is value non-users may be willing to pay for the preservation of the asset even if it is not used either today or in future. Non-use values pose a special challenge to valuation given that, by definition, existence value need not be revealed in any type of behaviour. The contingent valuation method, which directly asks willingness to pay through the use of surveys, is the only way to elicit such values (Bolt et al, 2005).

Bequest value refers to the value that one associates with passing on the benefits of an environmental resource to future generation. In other words, these values arise because of altruism towards future generations (Perman et al., 2003).

3.1.2 Valuation Methods

Valuation techniques have been developed and applied to measure natural resources' values so that economic impacts resulting from alterations of conditions influencing the flow of goods and services provided by these resources can be assessed. These valuation techniques may be grouped into three major categories. They are; Revealed Willingness to Pay, Circumstantial Evidence or Imputed Willingness to Pay and Expressed Willingness to Pay. In each of these categories, there are several alternative methods[11]:

- ➢ Revealed Willingness to Pay includes: Travel Cost Method (TCM), Random Utility Modelling (RUM), Averting Behaviour Method (ABM), Hedonic Pricing Method (HPM), Market Price Method (MPM) and Production Function Method (PFM).
- ➢ Circumstantial Evidence/Imputed Willingness to Pay includes: Replacement Cost Method (RCM), Substitute Cost Method (SCM) and Damage Cost Method (DCM).
- ➢ Express Willingness to pay method involves the using of Contingent Valuation Method (CVM) and the Choice Experiment Method (CEM).

3.1.2.1 Revealed Willingness to Pay

Revealed Willingness to pay method consists of exploiting the existence of a market price for an environmental good, in order to assess its economic value. It is argued that if the observable prices are not distorted, then the economic value of marginal environmental changes can be valued by directly using existing market prices.

However, if the natural resource of interest provides multiple goods and services, where some or all of them are unmarketable, this valuation approach will fail to provide reliable measures of the resources' value. This approach can only be used to measure use values (Mendelsohn and Olmstead, 2009) and considering the fact that the use values only

---

[11] Mishra, S. K. (undated) "Valuation of Environmental Goods and Services: An Institutionalistic Assessment". https://www.msu.edu/user/schmid/mishra.htm

represent a partial estimate of total economic value, estimates derived by revealed willingness to pay methods are only a lower bound estimates of TEV of a particular change in environmental quality. In the following sections, we review some of these methods.

3.1.2.1.1 Travel Cost Method (TCM)

The Travel Cost Method (TCM) was first proposed in a letter from Harold Hotelling to the US Forest Service in the 1930s. It was first used by Wood and Trice in 1958, and popularised by Clawson and Knetsch (1966). The underlying assumption of the TCM is that if an individual is willing to pay the cost of visiting a recreational site then he/she should value that site as much as what he paid to visit the site. Travel cost method relies on the assumption that people make repeated trips to recreational sites until the marginal utility derived from a trip equals the marginal cost of the trip. In other words, people's willingness to pay to visit the site can be estimated based on the number of trips they make at different travel cost. It is argued that, since many natural areas have low or no admission prices, TCM uses travel cost as a proxy for estimating consumers' surplus and extracting it via changes in admission fees. Thus, the basic premise of the TCM is that, time and transportation cost expenses that people incur to visit a site represent the price of access to the site.

The weak complementarity of the goods required to travel to the site makes it possible to estimate a demand curve for the site, and from it, a measure of the site's consumer surplus can be found. It is also important to note that the consumer surplus figure is a measure of the use value of the site only, and does not necessarily assume the site's environmental or intrinsic value. These travel cost can be regarded as a directly revealed preference for a recreation and an indirectly revealed preference for nature.

The travel costs are assumed to be related to distance. The first step of the TCM is the creation of trip generation function. The trip generating function links the visitation rate to its determinants including the cost of travelling plus any admission fees and all other determinants which is mostly the socioeconomic characteristic of the individual. The purpose of this function is to provide a model of the site use. There are two approaches:

> *Zonal travel cost method* - In order to estimate the WTP of visitors from various distances, distance circles are drawn in the service area of a site. This approach assumes that people from the same circle have homogeneous preferences. It is applied by collecting information on the number of visits to the site from different distances. Because the transportation and time cost will increase with distance, this information allows the researcher to calculate the number of visits purchased at different prices. Under the Zonal TCM, the visitation rate is obtained as the number of visits from any given zone divided by the population of that zone. The explanatory variables are the average values for the zone: average income, average age etc. This information is used to construct the demand function for the site, and estimate the consumer surplus or economic benefits for the recreational services of the site.
> *Individual travel cost method* - In this case the observation units are the individuals (or a sample of them) visiting the park. The visitation rate refers to the number of

trips made by any individual in a specified period. The explanatory variables refer to individual characteristics.

The validity of TCM can be doubted because people might not know the total pleasure or costs before they decide to go on a trip. Individuals may also combine a visit to a natural site with a family visit. This is known as a multipurpose trip and it does not help to accurately value the amount the individual spent in terms of time cost and transportation cost on the site. In other words, it is debatable whether the full travel cost to a recreation site may be attributed to nature, because these expenditures may not have been made purely for nature.

Moreover, the original conception of the TCM envisioned the cost of travel as being a sufficient explanation of people's willingness to pay for a recreational site. But the most perfunctory observations indicate that decisions about recreation are based in large measure not just on the cost of travel, but also on the availability of time. This suggests that one common approach to dealing with time costs by simply omitting them is inappropriate. One other response is to value time at a fixed percentage of the wage rate. This also raises the question of whether only the travel time should be accounted for, or whether on-site time should be included as well.

A bias of TCM it is argued concerns the representativeness of the sample. It is argued that, people who do not visit a site may still value the site, but they are excluded from the sample. This based on the weak complementarity assumption between environmental asset and consumption expenditure which states that if consumption expenditure is zero, then the marginal utility of the public good is also zero (Hanley et al. 2002). It is also argued that, people who really appreciate the site may have moved closer to the site and therefore have lower travel cost. Moreover, population distribution (close to/far from the site) has an impact on the demand for the recreation and thus on the valuation of the site. The strength of this impact depends on whether an individual is looking at the total value of the site or at the value per visit. Most technical problems with TCM relate to this (Stynes, 1990).

Furthermore, TCM can only capture part of the total economic value of nature. The recreational value is only part of the total value of nature since society does not derive welfare from nature through recreation. A consequence is the fact that TCM only reveals the welfare realised by the visiting population and therefore it can only measure use values (Hanley et al., 2002).

The TCM has often been applied to recreation, wetland visitation and hunting. Because of this, it is often difficult to conceive the validity of the TCM as a potential technique for the valuation of the demand for improved water supply service as in this study.

3.1.2.1.2 Random Utility Modelling (RUM)

The RUM is an extension of the travel cost method. It seeks to estimate recreational use values for individual features of a natural resource. This method can be useful where for instance; a potential development project causes damage to only some features of a recreational site in an area. The probability that an individual will visit a particular site A rather than site B is then estimated depending on the costs of visiting each site and their characteristics relative to the characteristics of all sites in the individual's choice set. The method can be used to estimate recreational use value of changing environmental quality of site attributes in addition to recreational use value of the site in total. Coyne and Adamowicz (1992) applied the method to the valuation of the site characteristics for alternative bighorn sheep hunting sites.

Some of the caveats of this method are that; it underestimates the total economic value since it can only estimate use values. Moreover, this method may have substantial data requirements. Problems may be encountered when dealing with multipurpose trips. This method cannot be used to predict changes in environmental quality without precedence. The method is also not suitable for this study because like the TCM, it is only suitable for the valuation of resources such as national parks, forests, public woodlands, wetlands etc.

3.1.2.1.3   Averting Behaviour Model (ABM)

Averting Behaviour Method is especially suited for valuing natural qualities. This is done by looking at expenditures made to avert or mitigate effects from the reduction of a natural quality. Typically, environmental hazards that results in averting and mitigating actions include water pollution, noise from airports or roads, air pollution, the extent of soil degradation in a rural area and ozone layer depletion. Averting Behaviour Method relies on the assumption that people perceive the negative effects of environmental deterioration on their welfare and that they are able to adapt their behaviour to avert or reduce these effects. For instance, this means that, people experience the negative effects of water pollution and that they spend resources on boiling, hauling and buying safe water in order to obtain this very necessary resource.

Analysing the decisions of individuals regarding the availability of clean water can provide useful information on the benefits derived from an investment in clean water supply. Therefore the willingness to pay for a clean environment is deduced from people's purchases of products and services to avert the negative effects of pollution.
Most applications of the ABM concern the purchase of protective items in relation to an environmental quality. For instance, people tend to buy hats and sun creams to prevent damage to their health by ozone depletion. As such, ABM is a cost-based method. This is because the cost of purchasing such items are used to value environmental qualities, even though the social preferences for a healthy environment may be much greater than the expenditures on those products. There has been applications of the ABM to value for example, the reduced risk of car accidents (Blomquist, 1979); the reduced risk of death as a result of fitting smoke alarms (Dardin, 1980) and the noise nuisance from airports (Layard, 1972). Since the market prices of the products are used to value the environment, ABM cannot capture the consumers' surplus.

The ABM is questionable in terms of validity because of the assumption that people actually purchase certain goods to protect themselves against environmental deterioration where in actual fact; people may make the purchase for the sake of the product and not to avert negative effects from their living environment (for instance, in the case of the sun cream, it would be very cheaper to stay away from the sun than to buy the sun cream). People buying such products actually mean that, they have less money to spend on the environment.

Moreover, one other concern associated with the use of ABM is that, people may not react to small changes in environmental quality. They may only react when a certain threshold has been passed. Besides that, one may argue that, such defensive purchases will not wipe out and will certainly not reverse the negative effects of environmental quality deterioration.

Furthermore, determining the value of a clean environment in terms of the expenses made to avert negative effects of environmental deterioration automatically introduces bias. That is, only the WTP of people who display certain averting or mitigating behaviour is measured, while people who behave differently may also have a WTP for a clean environment. The data requirements of ABM may be large, depending on the number of ways in which people try to avert the effects of an unhealthy environment. In addition to these problems, health-behaviour and health-environmental quality relations are difficult to determine and are not easy to verify in practice.

Averting Behaviour Method is mainly oriented toward health risks and therefore can only capture the value of certain attributes of nature (clean air in this case) but it cannot be used to determine the total economic value of nature. The ABM cannot be used to determine the non-use value of an environmental resource and therefore it cannot be a good method for this study.

3.1.2.1.4 Hedonic Pricing Method (HPM)

The hedonic pricing method is used to estimate economic values of ecosystem or environmental services that directly affect market prices. According to Anderson (1993), Hedonic price valuation tries to measure the value of a non-marketed economic component as a measurable component (attribute or characteristic) of a marketed good. The HPM may be traced back to the characteristic theory of value which was developed by Lancaster (1966) and it relies on the proposition that an individuals' utility for a good is based on its attributes. The basic principle of the HPM is that the price of a marketed good is related to its characteristics, or the services it provides. In other words, people value the characteristics of a good or the services it provides rather than the good itself. Thus, prices will reflect the value of a set of characteristics including environmental characteristics which people consider very important when purchasing a good.

For example, when buying a car, the individual is not interested in the car per se, but in its features such as comfort, style, speed, luxury, power, shape, fuel economy and so on. Also when buying or renting an apartment, the individual will usually consider its size, number of rooms, neighbourhood, distance from commercial centres, distance from public schools and so on. Therefore we can value the individuals characteristics of the car, house or any other good by looking at how the price people are willing to pay for it changes when its characteristics changes. Thus by modelling individuals' willingness to pay for a particular good as a function of its characteristics, hedonic pricing tries to pick up the impacts of changes in environmental service flows upon individuals' utility. The hedonic price method is often used in the context of property and labour markets. When the HPM is applied to value residential property it is called Property Value Approach and when applied to the labour market, it is called the Wage Differential Approach.

The HPM is relatively straightforward and uncontroversial to apply because it is based on actual market prices and fairly easily measured data. The HPM starts with a regression of house prices (or wages) against all their valuable characteristics. This leads to a hedonic price function of the following shape:
Value (house) = F (architecture, contents, neighbourhood, amenities, local taxes, harmful facilities, etc.).
From this function one can calculate the willingness to pay for a marginal change in each of these explanatory variables. This is the implicit price of the amenity under investigation. From these implicit prices, the demand curve for a specific amenity can be derived. The demand curve is then used for estimating the economic value of an amenity such as natural beauty.

The validity of the method may be questioned because it is possible that, in the case of valuing houses, there are several amenities that influence the price of a house in opposite directions. For example, there may be a positive influence of a park nearby, but at the same time, two noxious facilities which supply jobs. It is also possible that the house market is distorted due to governmental interventions (Pearce and Markandya, 1989). One other weakness of the HPM is the assumption of weak complementarity (which means that, if an individual does not use the marketed good, his/her WTP for the environment is zero) which implies that HPM may only estimate well-perceived changes of a property's neighbourhood's environmental characteristics and it does not estimate the impacts of environmental changes elsewhere.

Generally, the HPM is only able to provide value estimates of the impacts of environmental changes affecting the individual's WTP for private goods. In other words, HPM is intrinsically unable to estimate non-use values and is also incapable of estimating the impacts of changes in service flows underlying use values, which are not affected by the selected market good's price (de Boer et al., 1997).
The method is relatively complex to implement and interpret and also large amount of data must be gathered and manipulated. Statistical problems may also arise in HPM estimates. For example, a misspecification error which is related to the choice of the functional form for hedonic price function and omitted variable bias problems which relates to the choice of the function's argument. Multicollinearity which arises when there are two or more explanatory variables that are highly and not perfectly correlated with each other is also a potential statistical problem affecting HPM (Dosi, 2000). For example, some property's attributes such as neighbourhood socioeconomic variables may be highly correlated with each other, and some of these variables may be closely related with the environmental variable(s) of interest. Since the HPM cannot capture the non-use value of nature, it cannot be an appropriate method for our study.

3.1.2.1.5 Market Price Method (MPM)

The MPM estimates producer's surplus and consumer's surplus using market price and quantity data regarding the environment goods/services (example fish, timber etc.) traded in the market. Producer's surplus is the benefit that, the producer enjoys over and above the cost that he/she has incurred in producing and marketing the output. Similarly, consumer's surplus is the benefit enjoyed by the consumer over and above the cost that he/she has paid for commanding the goods. The total net economic benefit (economic surplus) is the sum of producer's surplus and consumer's surplus. Environmental goods and services that generate larger net surplus are more valuable.

This method has several caveats. One of the limitations of this method is that only a few environmental goods/services are bought and sold in the market and thus its coverage is limited. Moreover, market imperfections distort prices and therefore, the effectiveness of such prices in measuring the net benefit is questioned. Furthermore, the realm of market economy depends on the level of development of an economy. In less developed economies, many resources that contribute to the market go unaccounted and therefore are not reflected in the prices. Also, prices of environmental goods and services vary seasonally and cyclically.

The estimation of the net economic benefits depends on the estimation of producer and consumer surpluses, which in turn depends on the specifications of the demand and supply curves. Depending on the specification, the functional relationship between demand, supply and their determinants may be extremely complicated or too simple. The list of explanatory variables (such as income, prices of substitutes, prices of other goods, taste and preferences, etc.) may not be an easy task to make. As a result, the estimation of the producer as well as the consumer surplus will be model dependent and consequently making the estimated net benefit model dependent (Appau-Danso, 2004). The MPM cannot capture the non-use value of nature and therefore cannot be used for our proposed improved water supply system.

3.1.2.1.6 Production Factor Method (PFM)

The Production Function Method (which is also known as Change-in Productivity Approach or Effects on Production Approach) seeks to exploit the relationship between environmental attributes and the output level of an economic activity. Production Function Method is based on the fact that many natural resources, process and qualities are used as production factors. The underlying assumption of this method is that, an environmentally changing economic impact may be measured by considering the effects on production, and by valuing such effects at market output prices. In other words, the PFM tries to value natural qualities by valuing their impacts on production costs. An example of this relationship is the case of overgrazing which leads to soil erosion, and as the grass becomes patchy and the soil washed away, it reduces the soils capacity to sustain grass which animals graze thereby reducing the income accruing to the farmer. It is by focusing on this final impact of reducing farming income that the productivity approach can be used to value environmental degradation.

The PFM consists of two steps:
- ➤ The first step is aimed at identifying the physical impacts of environmental changes on a production activity.
- ➤ The second step consists of valuing these changes in terms of the corresponding change in the activities output.

The evaluation part of the PFM is mostly done by simply multiplying the quantity change by the market price. However, it would be better to investigate all economic effects such as changes in supply, demand and prices.

The approach can be used for a wide range of valuation problems. It has been widely used due to its ease of explanation and justification. The PFM can be applied to value the effects of water quality on agriculture, fishery industry, air pollution, crops and livestock and so on. In the case of crops and livestock, the PFM can be used to measure the decline in on-site crop yields caused by soil erosion, and the resulting downstream effects such as blockage of irrigation systems and sedimentation of reservoirs. Under air pollution, PFM can be used to determine the damage on human health resulting from air pollution and its impact on workdays. The method is meant to determine the changes in natural qualities on the economic production system. Consequently, it is not directly suited to determine the economic value of natural sites which are not cultivated.

The validity of the PFM is doubtful because of the fact that market prices are used to value certain environmental qualities. Production Function Method can only produce cost-based estimates of the value of the production capacity of nature and it does not include consumers' surplus when market prices are used. The costs of production losses may not cover the full social preference for nature.

It is very costly and relatively difficult to determine the environment-production linkages. This is due to the fact that co-operation is very much required between natural scientists, economists and other researchers in order to determine these linkages (Barbier, 1998).
The PFM has a large data requirement. This is because it is based on dose-response relations which involve a considerable amount of ecological information and because it requires economic data on natural products as well. In the case where one wishes to account for demand and supply dynamics, data requirements only become larger.

A bias of the PFM is that effects on production may have been distorted by averting behaviour. Producers will try to avert the effects of reduced natural qualities by undertaking all sorts of prevention activities, such as shifting to different crops or products, using of fertilizers, adapting cultivation or harvesting techniques etc.

Production Function Method allows one to determine the value of the production capacity of nature. For example, as waters are polluted (reduction of water quality), it reduces its capacity to sustain fish stocks and consequently reduces the income from fisheries. At the same time the polluted water may cause a rise in the production cost of drinking water (i.e increased treatment costs). The total economic value of nature does, however, comprise more attributes than fish production and water purification, and therefore the PFM can only capture part of the total economic value of nature. The PFM cannot capture the non-use value of nature and therefore cannot be a good measure of our proposed improved water supply system and therefore not suitable for our study.

3.1.2.2 Imputed Willingness to Pay Methods

Imputed Willingness to Pay methods (otherwise known as Circumstantial Evidence approach or Surrogate Market Valuation approach) consist of measuring the value of unmarketable environmental services by observing the market price (or the shadow price) of related economic goods and services. These related goods may include-substitute goods (these are goods which may replace environmental services or avoid/reduce the economic impacts of changes in service flow), environmental services' complementary goods and other marketable goods providing indirect information about environmentally changing economic impacts. These methods can be used to estimate people's willingness to pay based on the cost of actions they are willing to take, to avoid the adverse effects that would occur if these services are discontinued, or to replace the lost services or revive the service.

Three very closely related methods have been proposed that are based on these considerations[12]. They are:
- Replacement Cost Method,
- Substitute Cost Method, and
- Damage Cost Avoided Method.

Imputed willingness to pay method is based on the assumption that, if an individual incurs costs to avoid damages caused by lost to ecosystem services, or to replace the services of ecosystems, then these service must be worth at least what the individual paid to replace them. Thus, these methods are most approximately applied in cases where damage avoidance or replacement expenditures have actually been made.

The replacement cost method uses the cost of replacing an ecosystem or its services as an estimate of the value of the ecosystem and its services. In other words, the method takes as proxy the cost of replacing productive assets destroyed or rendered unproductive by the deterioration in environment quality. The cost of replacement is usually counted in terms of market values of physical replacements (e.g. cost of fertilizer to solve soil fertility loss).

The damage cost avoided method uses either the value of the property protected, or the cost of actions taken to avoid damages, as a measure of the benefits provided by an environmental resource.

The substitute cost method uses the cost of providing substitutes for an ecosystem or its services as an estimate of the value of the ecosystem or its services. For example, the flood protection services of a wetland might be replaced by a retaining wall or a levee. A typical example is the Keta[13] sea defence wall built to protect the people of Keta from the

---

[12] Mishra, S. K. (undated) "Valuation of Environmental Goods and Services: An Institutionalistic Assessment". https://www.msu.edu/user/schmid/mishra.htm
[13] a town in the Volta region of Ghana

possible flooding of the area by the sea. This cost of the sea defence wall can be used to value the Keta ecosystem.

This Surrogate Market Valuation technique is potentially capable of providing reliable welfare measures only if the value of the natural resource under consideration is revealed by related market behaviour and market prices. This may only occur for use values but never for non-use values. It therefore follows that if a resource does not provide benefits through its present (or expected) use, but because of its mere existence, the surrogate market valuation techniques are intrinsically unable to provide reliable value estimates. Moreover, these techniques assume that expenditures to repair damages or to replace ecosystem services are valid measures of benefits provided, where in actual fact costs are usually not an accurate measure of benefits. One other limitation of the Surrogate market valuation is that, the replacement cost method requires information on the degree of substitution between the natural resource and the market good and only a few of natural resources have such direct or indirect substitutes. These methods cannot capture the non-use value of nature and therefore cannot be used for our proposed improved water supply system.

3.1.2.3 Express Preference/Express Willingness to Pay Method

While the indirect market techniques described above can be used to value many of the benefits associated with environmental resource improvement, there are special cases in which they cannot be used. These indirect market techniques are most unlikely to value non-use values of environmental resources because they rely on data from situations where consumers make actual market choices such as travelling to visit a park (TCM), purchasing a house (HPM), using a fertilizer to solve soil fertility loss (replacement cost method) etc. and this may result in many errors (Gunatilake, 2003; Boardman et al., 1996; Hanemann, 1994; Hausman and Diamond, 1994). Freeman (1979) argued that, these indirect methods are just like detective work because they piece together sacrifices that people leave behind as they respond to other economic goals. These methods measure the expected consumer surplus rather than optional price and hence they give lower values because they only measure the use values of environmental resource.

This Express Preference approach (also known as the Stated Preference approach) consists of directly asking individuals which value they attach to unmarketable environmental services, and to express their preferences towards changes in service flows (Lareau and Rae, 1987). When this approach is applied in holistic way, it is potentially able to measure both use and non-use values and therefore a natural resource's total economic value. According to Mendelsohn and Olmstead (2009), the Stated Preference approach has the appealing virtue that it can be used to value any environmental good or service as long as the good can be described and because the approach is not tied to behaviour, it can be used to value some goods and services that revealed preference methods cannot value. This method is the survey method using the Contingent Valuation Method (CVM) and the Choice Experiment Method (CEM).

3.1.2.3.1 Contingent Valuation Method (CVM)

The contingent valuation method (CVM) for the valuation of environmental goods was first used by Davis (1963) in a study of hunters in Maine. However, it was only in the mid-1970s the method began to develop in earnest (Randall et al., 1974; Brookshire et al., 1976). Since then the method has become the most widely used and most controversial of all environmental valuation techniques (Hanley et al., 2002).

The Contingent Valuation method (CVM) is an approach that quantifies the value of an environment or society itself by calculating an amount that measures the WTP of local residents, or the amount of compensation required to agree to changing or eliminating the environment, and by replacing these amounts by pseudo prices. In other words, the CVM approach consists of directly asking individuals the value they attach to environmental resources and its attributes, and to directly state their preferences towards environmental changes. This process estimates the respondents' consumer surplus for the environmental good, and the maximum amount the non-marketed good is worth to the respondent.

It is explicitly done by explaining the effects and/or features of a certain environmental good and asking respondents in a surveyed interview or questionnaire: "How much do you think you (your household) can pay for the realisation of this environmental good at the maximum?" or "How much compensation would you (your household) expect if this environmental good cease to exist?" The value of the relevant environmental good is then estimated by multiplying the average values reported by the respondents by the total population (number of households). This is known as the open-ended contingent valuation format.

According to Desvousgas et al. (1983), respondents often find it difficult to assign a value spontaneously to a non-marketed good without some form of assistance and therefore many open-ended contingent valuation formats tend to produce an unacceptably large number of non-responses or protest zero responses to WTP questions. In other words, it is argued that asking respondents to give a monetary valuation in response to an open-ended question presents them with an extremely difficult task (Arrow et al., 1993).

The format of the closed-ended contingent valuation is a discrete/dichotomous choice question, where the respondent is presented with a value and gives a yes/no answer as to whether or not they would pay this amount. Their take-it-or-live it format mimics the choice facing buyers in an actual market or in the case of a public good, the choice facing citizens in a referendum. For this reason, the closed-ended contingent valuation formats (also known as referendum surveys) have become more popular as a technique for eliciting the value of environmental resources.

There are a few widely used elicitation techniques that attempt to overcome the weakness of contingent valuation in general, both in open-ended and closed-ended formats. These commonly elicitation methods are;
> **The Bidding game format:** the bidding game elicitation format requires the respondent to either go through a series of bids until a negative response is generated and a threshold established, or to select from a range of values. The

interviewer suggests the first bid (known as the starting point) and the respondents agree or disagree that they would be willing to pay (or accept) that price. The interviewer then iteratively increases the starting point price to see if the respondent would be willing to pay (or decreases the starting point price to see if the respondent would be willing to accept) for it until a negative response is given by the respondent for any extra increment (decrement) bid. The last accepted bid is then the maximum WTP (minimum WTA).

According to Cummings et al. (1986), the bidding game process is likely to capture the highest price consumers are willing to pay and thereby measuring the full consumer surplus. They also demonstrated that, starting point bias occur when the bidding game format is used.

➢ **The payment card format:** the payment card format was first developed by Carson and Mitchell (1981 and 1984) as an alternative to the bidding game. This is a more sophisticated direct questioning technique (which can be open or closed-ended) which specifies the increment or decrement in the value of the non-market good to be provided in quantitative terms. Furthermore, the payment card format avoids the need to provide a single starting point and it offers respondents more of a context for their bid than is provided in the direct questioning method. According to Carson and Mitchell (1989), this method is potentially vulnerable to biases associated with the ranges used on the cards and the location of the benchmark.

➢ **The Discrete Choice format:** the discrete choice format is also known as the take-it-or-leave-it format or the referendum format and it was developed by Bishop and Heberlein in 1979. This method requires the respondent to indicate approval or disapproval for a single monetary sum, which is varied across the interview sample. The most desirable form of the contingent valuation elicitation is the use of dichotomous questions that ask respondents to vote for or against a particular level of taxation as occurs in a true referendum. The rationale behind the discrete choice format is that most consumers are familiar with being confronted by a posted price for a good and the need to make decision to purchase at that price.

The main advantage of this method over other elicitation formats is that it simplifies the respondent's task in a fashion similar to the bidding game without having the iterative process. The respondent, just like any other consumer, has only to make a judgement about a given price.

The main limitation of this elicitation format relative to other formats is that more observations are needed for the same level of statistical precision in a sample WTP estimate because only a discrete indicator of a maximum WTP is obtained instead of the actual WTP amount.

➢ **The Discrete Choice with a Follow-up approach:** in this approach, respondents are required to answer a yes/no question regarding the WTP a specified price for an environmental good or service. If the respondent answers yes, another question is asked using a higher price randomly chosen from a pre-specified list. However, if the respondent answers no, a lower price is used in the follow up question.

Although this procedure offers potential for a considerable gain in efficiency, the inherent problems of discrete choice format still remains. Furthermore, the follow-up questions used in this method are similar to the iterative procedures of the bidding game hence suffering from some of the problems of the bidding game format.

The selection of elicitation design, however, depends on the type of good chosen to study and the structure of the market. The method selected to be used in this study is very much similar to the discrete choice with a follow-up approach.

Opponents of the contingent valuation methodology believe that, for a variety of reasons, respondents will not respond truthfully. They argue that misleading responses introduce bias into the survey and thus undermining the validity of the results.

Biases might arise at any stage of the CVM in the survey design and implementation: construction of the hypothetical scenario (Bishop and Heberlein, 1979); sample selection; development and application of the method and elicitation procedure for instance starting point bias in bidding games (Boyle et al., 1986; Thayer, 1981) and choice of bid vehicle (Rowe et al, 1980); or drawing inferences from the results. In order to overcome some of the biases involves careful survey and pretesting of questionnaires, competent management of the survey and enumerators, and the use of range of test and observations of the results during the analysis (Wedgewood and Sansom, 2003).

Some the biases that arise in the CVM include:

> **Strategic bias:** strategic biases arise when respondents intentionally understate their true WTP for the environmental good or service or deliberately exaggerate the amount they would be willing and could pay for the hypothetical good or service. Respondents might feel tempted to understate their true WTP in the hope of a free ride. Conversely, respondents might overstate their own ability to pay knowing fully that they could not afford that amount.
>
> In order to minimise the risk of strategic bias, the enumerator should make it clear to the respondent that there will be no subsidies in the case of higher strategic bids. According to Hoehn and Randall (1987), strategic bias can be reduced by using a referendum format (yes/no responses) to parametrically increasing amounts. They showed that truthful responses are always optimal in such a setting. Therefore the elicitation technique chosen will also help us to reduce the strategic bias.

> **Starting point bias:** starting point biases arise when the initial bid influences the final WTP given by the respondents. To be able to minimise the starting point bias, the initial bid should be varied within the sample frame to examine whether they are influencing the final WTP.

> **Interview and Compliance bias:** it is argued that the way enumerators conduct themselves can influence responses. This problem can be identified by separately analysing the responses of each enumerator and if it is found out that WTP is consistently higher or lower for all respondents interviewed by one particular enumerator, it is reasonable to infer that he/she somehow influenced the respondents to increase or decrease their bid. The results by that particular enumerator should be discarded.

Compliance bias arises when the respondent tries to guess the correct answer or tries to answer in a way that they think will please the enumerator. To be able to minimise this problem the enumerators should be well trained and they should be ensured to follow the exact wording of the questionnaire and not deviate from it.

> **Hypothetical bias:** hypothetical bias refers to the fact that the respondent does not understand or believe in the hypothetical market that has been developed. In order to minimise the level of misunderstanding, the options should be presented with a hypothetical scenario that is familiar to the respondent. Pictures and drawings will also help a great deal.

The main potential advantage of the CVM with respect to Revealed Preference valuation techniques, consists of its potential ability to provide estimates of both use and non-use values. One other advantage of the CVM is that, it is widely applicable and the only known technique for establishing the value of many non-market benefits (Pearce and Turner, 1990), in particular the non-use values of environmental goods which can be very significant (Pearce and Barbier, 2000). In fact, whilst Revealed Preference techniques measures only the environmental services' use value which can be inferred by looking at other related marketed goods, CVM is potentially capable of capturing the values derived from environmental attributes holding public features, which are not revealed by observable market behaviour (Mendelsohn and Olmstead, 2009). This is the main reason why the CVM is the technique being adopted by this study.

3.1.2.3.2 Willingness to Pay (WTP) versus Willingness to Accept (WTA)

The value attributed to contingent valuation methodology to a good or service can be studied from the perspective of compensating variation (the most the person would be willing to offer for a good to keep his/her utility constant), or equivalent valuation (the minimum amount required for an individual to forgo some good or to bear some harm). Compensating variation for an increase in a commodity q from q^0 to q^1 or equivalent variation for a decrease in the commodity from q^1 to q^0 can be defined using the individual's expenditure function. Compensating variation (WTP) and equivalent variation (WTA) are given by:

- $WTP = E(P, q^0, Q, U^0) - E(P, q^1, Q, U^0)$
- $WTA = E(P, q^1, Q, U^1) - E(P, q^0, Q, U^1)$

Where E denote the expenditure function, P the vector of prices for market goods, q the quantity of the non-market good consumed, Q a vector of other non-market goods and U^i the individual's utility when he consumes q^i.

Until recently, it was estimated in most practical situations that, the difference between WTP and WTA was small and negligible. This was shown in the words of Russell (1982) that states that, the difference between WTP and WTA in empirical studies is by chance and therefore should not be taken seriously.

In recent times, it is argued that the two measures may yield different values for the same commodity change. Willingness to pay for a good is usually many times lower than willingness to accept compensation to forego the same good (Hammack and Brown, 1974; Bishop and Heberlein, 1979; Rowe et al., 1980; Knetsch and Sinden, 1984; Hanley, 1998). Evidence suggests that people systematically value losses more highly than equivalent gains, and reductions in losses more highly than forgone gains (Knetsch, 1993).

The difference between the two measures for the same good or service has been widely studied through theory and experiment (Horowitz and McConnell, 2002). According to Hanemann (1991), the divergence between WTA and WTP can range from zero to infinity depending on the degree of substitutability between the goods and positive income elasticity. Hanemann argued that one should only expect convergence of WTP and WTA value measures when the good in question has a close substitute. When the good has an imperfect substitute, a value divergence will exist and will expand as the degree of substitution decreases.

Although WTA is the appropriate measure of value when the good that someone owns is damaged, it is often difficult to measure WTA accurately in contingent valuation surveys. Evidence of this is provided by the fact that willingness to accept compensation for quasi-private goods (hunting licenses) in contingent valuation surveys has been found to exceed actual willingness to accept compensation for the same goods (Bishop and Heberlein, 1979; Bishop et al., 1983). In view of these, researchers have focused almost exclusively on WTP as a measure of value in contingent valuation surveys since WTA question are often problematic as there are a lot of emotion involved in the answers. For instance if the individual already has the good initially and must give it up or in fact be "bribed" into giving it up, it results in high valuation statements.

3.1.2.3.3   Choice Experiment Method (CEM)

Choice experiment is similar to contingent valuation in that it can be used to measure both use as well as non-use values for virtually any ecosystem or environmental service. Unlike CVM, Choice Experiment does not directly ask respondents to state their WTP in monetary terms. Instead, the WTP is inferred from the hypothetical choices or trade-offs that people make.

In a Choice Experiment exercise, respondents are shown a set of alternative representations of a good and they are asked to pick their most preferred. Similar to real market situations, where consumers face two or more goods characterised by similar attributes but at different levels of these attributes, the respondents are asked to choose whether to buy one of the goods or none of them. In other words, Choice Experiments are a contingent valuation method based on random utility theory and Lancaster's characteristic theory of value which states that, the value of a good is determined by the attributes that make up the whole (Garrod and Willis, 1999).

Choice Experiment recognises that environmental impacts of development or policies are typically multi-dimensional with definable attributes combining to make up the whole, and attempts to elicit values for each of these attributes. This is achieved by offering respondents a choice of profiles made up of a combination of attributes including price. Respondents are then asked to choose any of the options or to retain the status quo-pay nothing and get nothing. The analysis of the trade-offs allows us to calculate the mean WTP for the different levels of each attribute.

The advantage of choice experiments is that they are more flexible and give greater information than a CVM for the whole, that the process does seem to mirror the kinds of decisions that are made in real life consumption decisions, that they seem more sensitive to scope (Hanley et al., 2001), and that they often offer a more diffuse focus on paying for the environment which reduces the incidence of protests (Pearce and Barbier, 2000).

3.2 Empirical Literature Review

Valuation techniques have been used extensively in the recent past to value environmental quality improvement and a variety of public programmes in developing countries. Until recently, the application of CVM was limited to developed countries. Few available works suggest that it can be successfully applied in developing countries as well (Appau-Danso, 2004; Adjei, 1999; Asenso-Okyere et al., 1997; Bah, 1997; Boadu, 1992; Jordan et al., 1993; Whittington et al., 1990).

With the rising awareness of the cost of environmental degradation in developing countries, coupled with pressures from donor organization about the inclusion of environmental impact assessment in project designs, valuation techniques are now being used extensively to evaluate the benefits of improved water supply, tourism and forestry projects.

In this review, we will briefly summarize water services related CVM from developing countries as well as those that have been done on other resources.

3.2.1 Willingness to pay: Improved Water Services

The World Bank water demand research team (1993) investigated the determinants of household demand for improved water services in some developing countries in Africa (Anambra State in Nigeria and Zimbabwe), Latin America (Brazil and Haiti) and South Asia (India and Pakistan).

The researchers used both the revealed preference (indirect method) and the stated preference (direct method) approaches to show how households made their choices about water supply systems. The indirect method used dichotomous choice econometric technique to derive household's decisions and estimate welfare change for the actual choice that households made. On the other hand, the direct method involves asking respondents how much they would be willing to pay for access to different kinds of water supply systems such as public taps and private water connections.

The findings that emerged from the studies revealed that, contrary to what was expected, WTP for improved water services does not depend solely on income. This is because they found out that income factor was statistically insignificant but it had the expected sign. The gender of the respondent proved to be statistically significant in the 11 surveys. They however concluded that its impact was strongly dependent on the specific cultural context. The studies also revealed that households will pay more for an improved water supply when cost in terms of time and money of obtaining water from existing source is higher than if such cost are low.

It was also revealed in the studies that if the perceived quality of the new improved water supply system is high, the WTP of households was always higher. Better-educated households were also more willing to pay for improved water supply services, and the effect of occupation, household size and composition of households on WTP was mixed. The researchers concluded that household's willingness to pay for improved water system is not dependent on anyone set of factors but rather on their joint effects. It is this joint effect that is modelled in the multivariate analysis.

Boadu (1992) employed the iterative bidding elicitation technique to examine the relationship between WTP for water and selected socioeconomic characteristics like household income, household size, education level of household, distance of water source from household, drought, ownership of household facilities and illness within thirty days of survey. A multiple regression was estimated using Ordinary Least Squares (OLS) from data collected from selected villages in Ghana. There was a positive relationship between household history of water related illness and the WTP for improved water services. The other socioeconomic factors effect did not follow any consistent pattern and therefore broad generalisations were not possible.

Using two equations and two estimation techniques (weighted OLS and Maximum Likelihood), Jordan and Elnagheeb (1993) employed the CVM to investigate people's WTP for improvement in drinking water quality in Georgia, USA. Their goal was to determine the influence of different socioeconomic and demographic factors on household's WTP. In the regression results, WTP was found to be positively related to the level of income and that the income elasticity of WTP was approximately 0.1. Willingness to pay was also found to increase with the level of education. Also female and younger respondents were found to be willing to pay more than their male and younger counterparts respectively. Furthermore, the results also indicated that on average, a private well owner was willing to pay more than an individual served by the public water system.

A study was conducted in America by Carson and Mitchell (1993) using the CVM to determine the national benefits of water pollution control. The regression results were reasonable in terms of signs and magnitude and they were all quite statistically significant. Based on the results, the policy recommendations were that, cost and benefits were roughly equal such that many of the new actions that were attempting to ensure all water bodies, at least a swimmable quality level could fail to yield positive benefits.

Aguilar and Sterner (1995) also used the CVM to investigate people's WTP for improved water services in three different study area which include; Guanacaste and Limon in Costa Rica and Muang Xiathani in Laos.

The main objective in Guanacaste was to determine the influence that different socioeconomic variables and characteristics of current water services have on WTP for improved water services by households. The empirical result indicated that WTP is positively influenced by income and age. Household size was found to be negatively related to WTP by households.

In Limon, a total of 300 households out of 1556 households in five villages were interviewed. The findings revealed that women on average were willing to pay more than men and young people are willing to pay more than older people.
In Muag Xiathani in Laos, a total of 300 households from seven villages were interviewed. The same data were collected as in Guanacaste and Limon. In this area, male respondents were found to have higher WTP for improved water services than females. Income and the size of the household were also found to have positive impacts on WTP by households.

In all, the results indicated that on average, inhabitants are willing to pay 80%, 40% and 71% over the current fees in order to receive improve water services in Guanacaste, Limon and Muag Xiathani respectively.

Bah (1997) employed both the CVM and HPM to estimate the WTP for improved water services in Freetown, Sierra Leone. The regression results from the CVM study showed that, gender, educational level, income, number of years in residence, expenditure on water and respondent attitudes towards water management have significant influence on WTP for an improved water supply service. The HPM results indicated that the size of the household and the expenditure on water are significant in determining the rental value of a house in Freetown.

Adjei (1999) used the CVM and the OLS econometric technique to determine the factors influencing the demand for improved water services in the Greater Accra Metropolitan Area (GAMA). A secondary data from a survey of 1000 household in 1991 was used. The following variables were used to estimate the model: income, education, time spent in collecting water, perception of water quality and distance from home to existing water source.

The empirical findings indicates that WTP is positively related to income, education, time spent in collecting water and distance from home to existing water source and it is negatively related to the perception of water quality. It also revealed that, people were willing to pay for improved water services per month in GAMA but what they were willing to pay was lower than the cost of production for the same period.

Calkins et al. (2002) estimated the WTP for improved drinking water delivery systems of 62 households in semi-urban area of Douentza, Mali. The linear regression model and the logit econometric model were used to estimate the WTP. The regression results revealed that wealth, relative distance to the proposed new sources compared with the best existing sources, land tenure security and family size are major determinants of respondent's WTP for improved delivery systems. The study also reported that land tenure insecurity discourages construction of one's own well and hence households tend to pay more for public water sources.

Appau-Danso (2004) used the CVM to estimate the WTP for improved water supply in the Asante Akim South District in Ghana. The study used the logit function to determine the relationship between WTP for improved water supply system and some socioeconomic characteristics (income, age of the respondent, size of household, level of education and occupation of respondents) and characteristics of the existing water source (distance from respondent's homestead to the existing water source, time spent to fetch water and problems with existing water source).

The empirical result was that income, age, household size, level of education, distance from the respondent's homesteads to the existing source and occupation all have positive relationship with WTP for improved water supply services but income and level of education were not statistically significant at 10% significant level. Time spent to fetch water from existing water source which was expected to have a positive impact was negative and it was statistically insignificant. The empirical result also indicates that people are willing to pay for an improvement in the provision of water in the area which will be able to sustain the company responsible for the production and supply of water in the area.

Using the logit model, Engel et al. (2005) estimated the determinants of improved water supply of households from two communities in the Ghanaian Volta Basin. The empirical result indicates that quality perceptions and distance to the improved and unimproved water source play an important role in household's choice of water source. The effect of prices and income levels on household choices differs according to the pricing system. Household's behaviour is sensitive to price charge relative to income if the per unit price is used but if the flat rate is charged, income level plays a more important role than price. Socioeconomic characteristics like age, sex and education level positively affects the decision to use improved water source. The result also indicated that the poorest, uneducated and the richest, highly educated segments of the communities are more likely to involve themselves in taking decision for improved water supply than the middle class.

Hensher et al. (2005) adopted the stated choice experiment method and the mixed logit econometric model to investigate households' WTP for water service attributes in Canberra, Australia. The regression results revealed that households are willing to pay more to reduce the frequency of the duration of water service interruptions and waste water overflows. Respondents also expressed a strong desire to have water service interruptions during the weekdays rather than weekends.

Fissha (2006) employed the CVM to estimate the determinants of households demand for improved water in Addis Ababa, Ethiopia. Two econometric models (tobit and probit) were used to investigate the relationship between WTP for improved water and some socioeconomic characteristic of households (income, education, sex, age, marital status, household size and respondents years of stay in the area) and the characteristics of the existing water source.

The regression result indicates that income, education level, age, sanitation facility, perceived water quality and water related disease have a significant impact on WTP for improved water services. Marital status and respondents years of stay in the area were found to have negative impact on WTP in the tobit model and they were also statistically insignificant but they were found to have a positive significant impact in the probit model.

Adepoju and Omonona (2009) used a multistage random sampling of 142 households in the Osogbo metropolis and the logit model to estimate the relationship between the WTP for improved water supply and some socioeconomic characteristics of households like age, level of education, household size, household expenditure (used as a proxy for income), connection charges and percentage of WTP from income. The results showed that the socioeconomic characteristics of households do not significantly influence willingness to pay for improved water supply but the percentage of income that a household is willing to pay for improved water supply and the willingness to pay for connection charges to the improved source are statistically significant at 10% significant level. However, age and education level are positively related to WTP for improved water sources.

Noor and Siddiqi (2009) adopted the CVM and the tobit econometric model to estimate the WTP for drinking water quality in Wasa, Lahore. The empirical results indicated that, household's willingness to pay is influenced by coping costs that households pay for ensuring quality of water. The study also showed that the education level of household head is an important factor in determining household's willingness to pay for improved water services.

Using the logistic (double-log) linear regression model, Olajuyigbe and Fasakin (2010) investigated the factors that influence people's WTP for improved sustainable water supply in a medium sized city in Southern Nigeria. The empirical results indicated that the most important determinants of water services in this area are: distance from main source to house, adequacy of supply from main source, quantity of water used per person per day, quantity of water purchased per day from vendor, average amount spent on water during dry season, main source of domestic water used by household, access to improved source of water, attack by water-borne diseases and performance of supply from the State Water Corporation.

3.2.2 WTP on Other Related Resources

Asenso-Okyere et al. (1997) used the CVM to estimate the WTP for health insurance by the informal sector in Ghana. Using the ordered probit model, the amount that households were willing to pay was found to be influenced by dependency ratio, income, sex, health care expenditure and education. The study also indicated that over 90% of respondents agreed to join the scheme and up to 63.6% of respondents were willing to pay a premium of $3.03 a month for a household of five persons.

In a study by Asafu-Adjaye and Dzator (2003), the CVM was used to evaluate the WTP for malaria insurance in Ghana. The regression results indicated that WTP was significantly influenced by income, years of formal education, occupation and the number of children in the household.

A contingent valuation study was done by Frick et al. (2003) to estimate household WTP for azithromycin treatment for trachoma control in Tanzania. The ordered probit regression analysis indicated that 38% out of the 394 households interviewed were not willing to pay for azithromycin treatment although they were willing to participate in the treatment.

Afroz et al. (2005) used different elicitation formats (open ended, discrete choice and payment card method) to estimate the WTP for air quality improvement in the Klang Valley, Malaysia. The results of the study suggested that the WTP values of the respondents do not differ significantly across different elicitation formats and that the WTP values for the respondents using the discrete choice format were the highest.

Rodriguez et al. (2007) adopted the CVM to estimate the WTP for organic food in Argentina. The binomial multiple logistic regression model was used to estimate the parameters of selected products. The results indicated that consumers were willing to pay a price premium to acquire better quality product condition on the effective prices in the domestic market.

Asfaw et al. (2008) adopted the double bounded CVM to estimate the WTP for health insurance in Namibia. The probit econometric model was used and the regression results indicated that the young were more likely to join the scheme than the elderly. The income variable was found to be statistically insignificant in explaining the decision of the respondent to join the scheme. However, education plays a statistically significant role in determining the decision of respondents to join the scheme.

Based on various studies that have been carried out in both developed and developing countries, the CVM has shown promise as a potential tool for investigating the economic benefits of the provision of non-marketed goods such as improved water services, good sanitation, health insurance and air pollution. The literature also shows that the decision of the potential users of improved water supply system depends on various factors like income, gender, education, time spent to fetch water from existing source, perceived quality of existing water supply, marital status and so on.

There are obvious dangers inherent in designing water supply systems without reasonable information on what services people want and for what they are willing to pay. This study will therefore use the CVM to elicit the value a typical household in the Accra-Tema metropolis places on an improved water service; based on materials from the literature that are consistent with the conditions of a developing country like Ghana.

CHAPTER FOUR

METHODOLOGY

This study seeks to elicit from households their willingness to pay for improved water supply using the Contingent Valuation Method (CVM). The CVM was first proposed by Ciriacy-Wantrup (1947) as a method for eliciting market valuation of a non-market good. The first practical application of the technique was done by Robert K. Davis in 1963 where he used surveys to estimate the value hunters and tourists place on a particular wild area. Currently, it is widely used to evaluate non-market goods and environmental resources. Contingent Valuation Method uses survey questions to elicit from a sample of consumers their WTP for improvement in environmental quality and\or their Willingness to Accept (WTA) for environmental deterioration. Information gathered through CVM depends on developed hypothesis.

Contingent Valuation Surveys excite a market for a non-marketed good or an environmental good and obtain a value for that good contingent on a hypothetical market scenario. In our case this means that we will carry out a house-to-house survey and ask users a range of questions about their existing water supply system in addition to other socioeconomic factors and then present a hypothetical scenario of an improved water supply. Respondents will be asked how much they will be willing to pay for the service.

4.1 Survey Instrument

The main survey instrument for the primary data collection was a questionnaire, which was administered to households in identified areas in the Accra-Tema metropolis through on-site face-to-face interviews. The most important part of the survey was the creation of a realistic contingent valuation scenario, which has accurately priced water supply options to reflect the levels of prices that the water provider would have to charge in order to provide the service. In creating the scenario, respondents were effectively asked what price they would be willing to pay for the water based on the level, quantity and quality of the water. The process was thoroughly supervised by the researcher with expert advice from supervisors.

4.2 Pilot Survey, Pretesting and Training

Opponents of Contingent valuation methodology argue that respondents do not answer questions accurately and thus invalidate their answers. Thus, it is essential for the researcher to develop realistic and practical scenarios with real options that have been carefully priced and that are likely to be familiar to the respondent. Hence we visited the designated sample areas, meeting residents in the area. By so doing, it enabled us to understand the current water supply situation before the questionnaire was designed. In order to pre-test the questionnaire respondents were invited to answer as many questions they possibly could, skipping those they believed to have no knowledge of. This approach helped the researcher to gauge the time needed to complete the questionnaire, assess the clarity and the level of difficulty of the questions. Results from the pilot survey were used to review and update the questions.

A training course was organized for interviewers who are undergraduate students from the University of Ghana. The training instructed the interviewers on the level of information that constitute an adequate response for each question. The training was also used to teach the enumerators how to conduct the interview to avoid strategic behaviours. The principal training documents used were the questionnaire and field manual. This helped equip the enumerators with the rudimentary skills in administering the questionnaire.

4.3 Sample Frame

The study was conducted in the Accra-Tema metropolis. The metropolis was purposely selected because of the growing population and the numerous problems associated with the supply of water. A total of 340 households were drawn from the population using a two stage sampling technique. In all, 30 enumerators were employed by the researcher to do the survey.

In the first stage, the population was stratified into two: areas with critical[14] water supply problems and areas where water supply problems were believed not to be serious[15]. Areas with critical water supply problems were areas where water flows at most two days in a week and up to five hours in a day. The simple random sampling technique was then used to select the households interviewed in these two strata in the second stage.

The enumerators were grouped into 10 separate groups with a group having either 3 or 4 members. Each group was sent to a particular area in the two strata and each enumerator is supposed to choose any household at random to be interviewed. In order not to interview the same household by different enumerators, they enumerators were to work in a group. The survey took place on a Saturday and it started from 09:00GMT to 17:30GMT.

4.4 Design Survey Questionnaire and Elicitation Format

The design of the contingent valuation questionnaire was done based on the following recommendations by the National Oceanic and Atmospheric Administration (NOAA) in 1994. The most important points were that: the hypothetical facts provided to the respondents should be precise, understandable and constant across sample; WTP should be about a future event and not an event that has already occurred; and the interview should be conducted in person. The panel argued that it is important to clearly and precisely define the hypothetical good or service being offered to people in order to obtain the correct WTP values. It is therefore necessary to be specific about the environment benefits of the proposed new improved service since that is what the individual is really paying for. Following these suggestions by the panel, the possibility of getting wrong and inconsistent responses is minimised or eliminated.

The household interview included questions about the characteristics of existing water use conditions and problems, the existing sanitation practice, households WTP for improved water services and the socioeconomic characteristics of households. In order to

---

[14] Adenta, Madina, Haatso, Dome, Accra New Town.
[15] Achimota, Awoshie, Tema, Dansoman, Mempeasem.

minimize the strategic responses by respondents, the following statement was initially read to all respondents before the interview is conducted:

> Hello, I am _____, a research enumerator from the University of Ghana assisting in data collection for an on-going research by Mr. Ebo Botchway in partial fulfilment for the award of Master of Philosophy Degree in Economics. We are interviewing a sample of households in the Accra-Tema metropolis with the aim of estimating the WTP for improved water supply in the Accra-Tema metropolis. Please be assured that information provided would not in any way be linked to you and would be treated with utmost confidentiality. This interview is completely confidential and strictly for academic purposes and therefore honest discussion is the best way ahead.

The main focus of the questionnaire was to estimate the household's willingness to pay for improved water supply system. The elicitation format adopted for this study is the discrete choice with a follow-up approach. This format was chosen because it helps to minimise the strategic bias and make the decision most efficient. This format also helps to minimise starting point bias which much is prevalent in other elicitation formats.

4.5 Field Operations

The field work began in the first week of January, 2011 and it continued for about three weeks. The task of the interviewers was to randomly identify households in the area they are sent to, explain the purpose of the survey, conduct interview and review the completed questionnaire. The work of the supervisor was to review the completed questionnaire for completeness, consistency and accuracy, and to coordinate the work of the interviewers to ensure that the desired information is obtained. The supervisor also monitored and controlled the fieldwork and made adjustments where necessary to individual interviewer's workloads. Interviewers were also asked to enter their itineraries and appointments on planning forms. This was also reviewed by the supervisor.

4.6 Data Analysis

The data was analysed using STATA econometric software and the relevant information was obtained through sorting and cross-tabulation queries. Double data entry was also employed to make it easy to check errors in data captured.

Responses from the CVM survey was analysed by estimating the mean WTP bids from the sample and expanding it across the population to obtain the aggregate WTP for improved water supply which invariably serves as a measure of the cost of inadequate and poor quality water supply.

A qualitative choice of willingness to pay was regressed on the socio-economic factors and other attributes of existing and proposed improved water supply. This has helped us to identify the significance factors that influence household's willingness to pay for improved water supply in the metropolis.

4.7 Theoretical Framework

Contingent Valuation Method assumes that households are aware of the problems facing them as a result of poor water supply service and therefore will be willing to bear the cost of improved water supply. The independent variables and the amount that households would be willing to pay will be analysed using the Ordered Probit econometric model.

Consider a Random Utility Model in which utility U_{ij} provided to individual i by good j is composed of a deterministic component V_{ij} which can be calculated based on observed characteristics and a stochastic error component ε_{ij} which is unobserved. The indirect utility function for the jth respondent can be specified as:

$$U_{ij} = U_i\left(Y_j, X_j, \varepsilon_{ij}\right)$$

Where Y_j is household j^{th} disposable income, X_j is the vector of observable household characteristics and attributes of a given choice, ε_{ij} is the unobservable random component of the given indirect utility and i represent the choice response of the respondent, $i=1$ denotes "yes" response and $i=0$ denotes "no" response.

A payment bid (Y_i^*) is introduced which changes the measurable attributes like quality and quantity of the environmental good in the CV survey. The consumer will accept the proposed payment only if the utility derived from the final state (improved state) is greater than the utility derived from the initial state (status quo). That is when

$$U_{ij}\left(Y_j - Y_i^*, X_j, \varepsilon_{ij}\right) > U_{ij}\left(Y_j, X_j, \varepsilon_{ij}\right)$$

Where Y_i^* is the amount the respondent is willing to pay for the proposed improved system. The random components of preferences cannot be observed and therefore only probability statements of "yes" or "no" can be made. Thus the probability that the respondent answers "yes" is an indication that the respondent is better off in the proposed program. Therefore for the jth respondent, the probability that he/she answers "yes" is given by:

$$\Pr(yes) = U_{1j}\left(Y_j - Y_i^*, X_j, \varepsilon_{1j}\right) > U_{0j}\left(Y_j, X_j, \varepsilon_{0j}\right)$$

This probability statement provides an intuitive basis to analyse binary responses. One of the common formulations of the RUM is the Additive RUM (ARUM). Under ARUM, it is assumed that the utility function is additively separable into deterministic and stochastic preferences (Cameron and Trivedi, 2005), i.e., $U_{ij}=U_i(Y_j, X_j) + \varepsilon_{ij}$. Therefore the probability statement becomes:

$$\Pr(yes) = U_{1j}\left(Y_j - Y_i^*, X_j\right) + \varepsilon_{1j} > U_{0j}(Y_j, X_j) + \varepsilon_{0j}$$

4.7.1 The Ordered Probit model

Although the value households place on the proposed water supply system is a continuous variable, it is believed that the most reliable data that will be generated from the discrete choice with a follow-up elicitation format are the set of yes/no responses to questions about specific, discrete prices. For example, households accepting to pay an amount GH¢Y_0 as their maximum WTP may actually be willing to pay a higher amount not exceeding GH¢Y_1 (>GH¢Y_0). That is, although a response may not necessarily be the maximum WTP; the "true" WTP may lie in the interval between the maximum value the respondent is willing to pay and the next highest value (Maddala, 1983; Greene, 2008). In other words the observed dependent variable obtained from the discrete choice with a follow-up elicitation procedure is not the maximum amount the household is willing to pay but, rather, an interval within which the true willingness to pay falls (Whittington et al., 1990).

The implication of this is that although the outcome of the event is discrete, the multinomial logit or probit model would fail to account for the ordinal nature of the response variable. The ordered probit model has merits over the unordered multinomial conditional or nested logit or probit models. This is because, while accounting for the nature of the dependent variable, the unordered multinomial probit and logit models fail to account for the ordinal attribute of the dependent variable (Duncan et al., 1998). The multinomial logit models have further been criticised as having undesirable attributes such as the famous independence of irrelevant alternatives (IIA) whereas the multinomial probit suffers from a closed-form likelihood function (Greene, 2008). As an example, Greene shows that the odds ratio between car and bus passenger numbers changes if one further differentiates cars into domestic and foreign makes and models.

Linear regression model is also not an appropriate procedure for dealing with such an ordinal dependent variable because the assumptions regarding the specification of the error term in the linear model will be violated (Maddala, 1983). The ordered probit is preferred to the linear regression model since it accounts for the unequal differences between ordinal categories in the dependent variable (Greene, 2008; Duncan et al., 1998). For instance, the ordered probit model does not assume that the difference between the bids "Not WTP" and "WTP a lower price" is the same as the difference between "WTP a moderate price" and "WTP a higher price" and thereby capturing the qualitative differences between the rates that households are willing to pay. Also like the OLS, the ordered probit model accounts for the statistical significance between the dependent and the independent variables (Duncan et al, 1998).

Therefore, in this case, the more appropriate estimation model would be the ordered probit model. In the next paragraphs we explain how the model works.

Let WTP_i^* be the maximum amount household i is willing to pay for the proposed water supply system. Based on consumer demand theory, WTP_i^* is hypothesized to be a function of the household's socioeconomic characteristics and the attributes of the new and existing water supply systems (Whittington et al., 1990). The ordered probit model is specified as follows:

$$WTP_i^* = \alpha + X_i'\beta + \varepsilon_i$$

Where X_i is a vector of the household's characteristics and attributes of the existing and the proposed improved water supply system, β is the vector of parameters of the model, α is the constant parameter and ε_i is the unobserved characteristic of the household. ε_i is the random error term and assumed to have a standard normal distribution. That is, it has a zero mean and a variance equal to one.

WTP_i^* is not observed from the bidding game and therefore it cannot be estimated. However, we would know the ranges within which WTP_i^* will fall from the responses. Let $R_1, R_2, \ldots, R_J$ be the j prices which divide the range of willingness to pay space into J+1 categories and let WTP_i be the categorical variable such that;

$$WTP_i = \begin{cases} 1 & \text{if} \quad WTP_i^* \leq R_1 \\ 2 & \text{if} \quad R_1 < WTP_i^* \leq R_2 \\ 3 & \text{if} \quad R_2 < WTP_i^* \leq R_3 \\ \cdot \\ \cdot \\ J+1 & \text{if} \quad R_J < WTP_i^* \end{cases}$$

Let j=1, 2,..., J+1. Therefore we have $WTP_i^* = j$ if

$$R_{j-1} < WTP_i^* \leq R_j$$
$$\text{or } R_{j-1} < \alpha + X_i'\beta + \varepsilon_i \leq R_j$$
$$\text{or } R_{j-1} - \alpha < X_i'\beta + \varepsilon_i \leq R_j - \alpha$$
$$\text{or } R_{j-1} - \alpha - X_i'\beta < \varepsilon_i \leq R_j - \alpha - X_i'\beta$$

The willingness to pay values obtained from the contingent valuation survey would be used as the dependent variable in the regression. This is because, although WTP_i^* is unobserved, we can determine the exact category of WTP it belongs to because each respondent in the sample would indicate the amount his/her household would be willing to pay for the proposed improved water supply system. The probability of household i choosing category j is given by;

$$\begin{aligned} P_i(j) = \Pr[WTP_i = j] &= \Pr\left[R_{j-1} < WTP_j \leq R_j\right] \\ &= \Pr\left[R_{j-1} < \alpha + X_i'\beta + \varepsilon_i \leq R_j\right] \\ &= \Pr\left[R_{j-1} - \alpha - X_i'\beta < \varepsilon_i \leq R_j - \alpha - X_i'\beta\right] \\ &= \Pr\left[\mu_{j-1} - X_i'\beta < \varepsilon_i \leq \mu_j - X_i'\beta\right] \\ &= \Phi\left[\mu_j - X_i'\beta\right] - \Phi\left[\mu_{j-1} - X_i'\beta\right] \end{aligned}$$

where $\mu_j = R_j - \alpha$.

Given that we have J+1 categories, the probability of household i choosing category j (=1, 2,..., J+1) is given by the following expressions (Wooldridge, 2002):

$$P_i(1) = \Pr(WTP_i = 1) = \Pr(WTP_i^* \leq R_1) = \Pr(X_i'\beta + \varepsilon_i \leq \mu_1) = \Pr(\varepsilon_i \leq \mu_1 - X_i'\beta)$$
$$= \Phi(\mu_1 - X_i'\beta)$$

$$P_i(2) = \Pr(WTP_i = 2) = \Pr(R_1 < WTP_i^* \leq R_2) = \Pr(\varepsilon_i \leq \mu_2 - X_i'\beta) - \Pr(\varepsilon_i \leq \mu_1 - X_i'\beta)$$
$$= \Phi(\mu_2 - X_i'\beta) - \Phi(\mu_1 - X_i'\beta)$$

$$\vdots$$

$$P_i(j) = \Pr(WTP_i = j) = \Pr(R_{j-1} < WTP_i^* \leq R_j) = \Phi(\mu_j - X_i'\beta) - \Phi(\mu_{j-1} - X_i'\beta)$$

$$\vdots$$

$$P_i(J) = \Pr(WTP_i = J) = \Pr(R_{J-1} < WTP_i^* \leq R_J) = \Phi(\mu_J - X_i'\beta) - \Phi(\mu_{J-1} - X_i'\beta)$$
$$P_i(J+1) = \Pr(WTP_i = J+1) = \Pr(WTP_i^* > R_J) = 1 - \Phi(\mu_J - X_i'\beta)$$

μ_j's are threshold parameters which are unknown parameters to be estimated in addition to the coefficient vector β. $\Phi[.]$ is the cumulative standard normal distribution (Greene, 2008). These threshold parameters (μ_j's) correspond to the cut-offs where an individual moves from reporting one category to another. The parameters β and the j threshold parameters are obtained by maximising the log likelihood function:

$$\ln L = 1[WTP_i = 1]\ln\left[\Phi(\mu_1 - X_i'\beta)\right] + 1[WTP_i = 2]\ln\left[\Phi(\mu_2 - X_i'\beta) - \Phi(\mu_1 - X_i'\beta)\right] + ..$$
$$......+ 1[WTP_i = j]\ln\left[\Phi(\mu_j - X_i'\beta) - \Phi(\mu_{j-1} - X_i'\beta)\right] + ... + ..$$
$$......+ 1[WTP_i = J+1]\ln\left[1 - \Phi(\mu_J - X_i'\beta)\right]$$

Simplifying this expression we have:

$$\ln L = \sum_{i=1}^{N}\sum_{j=1}^{J+1} WTP_{ij} \ln\left[\Phi(\mu_j - X_i'\beta) - \Phi(\mu_{j-1} - X_i'\beta)\right]$$

In the ordered probit model, the interpretation of the parameters is of less importance. This is because we are not very much interested in the response probability $\Pr(WTP|X)$ since WTP^* is unobserved and also an abstract construct (Wooldridge, 2002). Therefore for us to be able to analyse the results from the ordered probit model for policy making, it is necessary to estimate the marginal effects to show how the probability of each outcome changes with respect to changes in the explanatory variable. The equation for marginal effects for each category is given by:

$$\frac{\partial \Pr(WTP_i = 1 | X)}{\partial X_i} = -\phi(\mu_1 - X_i'\beta)\beta$$

$$\frac{\partial \Pr(WTP_i = 2 | X)}{\partial X_i} = [\phi(\mu_1 - X_i'\beta) - \phi(\mu_2 - X_i'\beta)]\beta$$

$$\vdots$$

$$\frac{\partial \Pr(WTP_i = j | X)}{\partial X_i} = [\phi(\mu_{j-1} - X_i'\beta) - \phi(\mu_j - X_i'\beta)]\beta$$

$$\vdots$$

$$\frac{\partial \Pr(WTP_i = J | X)}{\partial X_i} = [\phi(\mu_{J-1} - X_i'\beta) - \phi(\mu_J - X_i'\beta)]\beta$$

$$\frac{\partial \Pr(WTP_i = J+1 | X)}{\partial X_i} = \phi(\mu_J - X_i'\beta)\beta$$

where $\phi(.)$ is the derivative of $\Phi[.]$.

The signs of the marginal effects may differ from the sign of the estimated coefficient in the ordered probit model since the standard normal probability distribution function is symmetric about zero, increasing one of the explanatory variables while holding the parameters and the threshold constant is equivalent to shifting the distribution slightly to the right which will move some mass from out of negative to positive (Greene, 2008). As Greene put it, relative to the signs of the coefficients, only the signs of the changes in $\Pr(WTP_i=1|X)$ and $\Pr(WTP_i=J+1|X)$ are unambiguous.

4.8 Model Specification

The study proposes to estimate the following equation based on the theoretical framework discussed.

$$MWTP_i = \alpha + \beta_1 INC_i + \beta_2 ECW_i + \beta_3 TSWS_i + \beta_4 HSIZ_i + \beta_5 SEX_i + \beta_6 BEDU_i + \beta_7 SEDU_i + \beta_8 TEDU_i + \beta_9 YRSA_i + \beta_{10} PQEW_i + \beta_{11} REL_i + \beta_{12} IB_i + \beta_{13} SATN_i + \beta_{14} MRS_i + \varepsilon_i$$

Where MWTP = Maximum Willingness to Pay
        INC = Monthly Income of Respondent.
        ECW = Existing or Current Cost of water.
        TSWS = Time Spent in fetching water from current access point of water.
        HSIZ = Number of individuals in the household.
        SEX = Sex of Respondent.
        EDU = Education level of Respondent.
               (BEDU = Basic Education; SEDU = Secondary Education; and TEDU = Tertiary Education).

YRSA = Respondents' Years of stay in the Area.
PQEW = Perceived Quality of Current Water Supplied.
REL = Reliability of Existing Water Supply Source.
IB = Initial Bid.
SATN = Sanitation Facility of Respondents.
MSR = Marital status of Respondents.

4.8.1 Description of Explanatory Variables

Income of Respondents (INC):
This continuous variable is a sum of the household head's income and the income of other members of the family. Empirical evidence shows that WTP for improved water services does not depend solely on income, but it depend equally on the characteristics of both the existing and improved services. A positive relationship is expected between income and willingness to pay for improved water supply.

Existing or Current Cost of Water (ECW):
This is a continuous variable and it measures households current cost of acquiring water for domestic use per month. Basic consumer demand theory suggests that households would pay more for an improved water supply when cost in time and money of obtaining water from existing sources are higher than if these cost were lower. Therefore there is a positive relationship between WTP and Existing Cost of Water (ECW).

Time Spent in fetching water from current access point of water (TSWS):
The longer the time spent in fetching water from the existing access point, the more time is wasted in doing other productive activities and thus the more households will be willing to pay for improved services. Therefore a positive relationship is expected. This variable is a continuous variable and it was measured in minutes.

Number of Individuals in the Household (HSIZ):
Household size is also a continuous variable which measures the number of people in the household. The effect of the size of a household on WTP for improved water supply is uncertain. As one study have shown that when there is an increase in the size of a household, the household will be more aware of the risk involved with poor water provision and thus the household will feel a better desire for better service, thereby giving a higher WTP. However, due to limited job opportunities in developing countries, as the size of the household increases, the number of unemployed members also increases. This will increase households' expenditure and a growing need to match the households' income. Thus households will have a low WTP as households' size increases in this case.

Sex of Respondent (SEX):
Usually, women almost universally bear the burden of collecting water. Therefore sociologist who study water use hypothesize that women would attach more importance to improved water supplies than would men and therefore be more willing to pay more for such improvements. But in many cultures women do not have equal control over or access to households' cash resources and therefore it is not clear how gender would

influence the respondents' indicated WTP for improved supplies. Sex is a dummy variable with male represented by 1 and female represented by 0.

Level of Education of Respondent (EDU):
Households with increased level of education would be more aware of the health benefits of improved water supplies and would therefore be more likely to use improved services if they are available, so one would expect that households with higher education levels would be willing to pay more to obtain improved services than households with lower educational levels. Moreover, because better or higher educated households might for a variety of reasons, have higher opportunity costs for time spent collecting water from sources outside house, they might well be willing to pay more for improved supply than other households with low levels of education. A positive relationship is thus expected between education and willingness to pay for improved water supply. Education will be categorised into No Education represented by 0, Basic Education (BEDU) represented 1, Secondary Education (SEDU) represented by 2 and Tertiary Education (TEDU) represented by 3.

Respondents' Years of Stay in the Area (YRSA):
It is hypothesized that if a household has been staying in a particular area for a long time, the household will be more willing to pay the proposed improvements since they will know more about the problems of the existing water supply services and therefore know more about the benefits that they would derive from the proposed improved water supply service. There will also be some sentimental attachments to the area. A positive relationship is thus expected.

Perceived Quality of Existing Water Supplied (PQEW):
Households would be willing to pay more for an improved water supply when the perceived quality of the existing or an alternative water source is poor. Perceived quality of water is considered to be a dummy variable with good quality represented by 1 and poor quality represented by 0. A negative relationship is thus expected.

Reliability of Existing Water Supply Source (REL):
Households will be willing to pay much more if the current supply of water from the existing source is deemed unreliable. Reliability is dummy variable with reliable represented by 0 and unreliable represented by 1. Thus a positive relationship is expected.

Initial Bid (IB):
This is done to see whether households' responses are very much affected by the initial bid. The relationship is due to be known in the course of the study.

Sanitation Facility of households (SATN):
Sanitation facility of households in this case refers to only the use of toilet facility by households and improved sanitation refers to the use of flush toilet. There are five sanitation facilities available in the Accra-Tema metropolis that would be selected. They are: Flush toilet, pit latrine, public toilet, bush and streets. Sanitation Facility of households is considered to be a dummy variable with one given to flush toilet and, 0

otherwise. A positive sign is expected because flush toilet requires the use of water for its function as compared to other sanitation facilities and hence makes households more willing to pay for the improved water service.

Table 4.1 Deterministic Statistics of the Explanatory Variables

Variable	Classification	Expected Sign	Mean	Std. Dev.	Min	Max
Monthly Income of Respondents (INC)	Continuous	+	1001.17	876.511	100	6000
Existing or Current Cost of water (ECW)	Continuous	+	41.14	21.366	8.8	130
Time Spent in fetching water from current source (TSWS)	Continuous	+	38.71	24.208	2	180
Number of individuals in the Household (HSIZ)	Continuous	+/-	5.15	2.363	1	16
Sex of Respondent (SEX) (Male=1; Female=0)	Dummy	+/-	0.51	0.501	0	1
Education level of Respondent (EDU) (No Education=0; Basic=1; Secondary=2; and Tertiary=3)	Categorical	+	1.86	0.915	0	3
Respondent's Years of stay in the Area (YRSA)	Continuous	+	8.79	8.319	0.25	50
Perceived Quality of Current water supplied (PQEW) (Good quality=1; and Poor quality=0)	Dummy	-	0.2	0.4	0	1
Reliability of Existing water supply source (REL) (Unreliable=1; Reliable=0)	Dummy	+	0.33	0.47	0	1
Initial Bid (IB)	Continuous	+/-	0.098	0.014	0.08	0.12
Sanitation Facility of Respondent (SATN) (Flush toilet=1;Otherwise=0)	Dummy	+	0.4	0.491	0	1
Marital Status of Respondent (MSR) (Married=1; Otherwise=0)	Dummy	+	0.69	0.464	0	1

Marital Status of Respondent (MSR):

This is a dummy variable taking 1 if the respondent is married; 0 otherwise. This variable is expected to have a positive sign since married people are more cautious of the health and other risk involved in poor water supply service due to family responsibility than their single, divorced and widowed counterparts.

CHAPTER FIVE

EMPIRICAL RESULTS AND DISCUSSION

This chapter deals with the empirical findings and discusses the results obtained from the contingent valuation survey. The data collected from the contingent valuation survey is analysed in two ways. The first part uses descriptive analysis with the help of cross tabulation between WTP and socioeconomic characteristics of the respondents and the second part deals with the econometric analysis of the data.

5.1 Descriptive Analysis

This section deals with the analysis of the socioeconomic characteristics of households, respondents ranking of social services, the characteristics of existing water use conditions and problems. It also deals with the analysis of the characteristics of the existing household sanitation practice.

5.1.1 Socioeconomic Characteristics of the Surveyed Households

As stated previously, a total of 340 households were interviewed from different areas of the Accra-Tema metropolis in the contingent valuation survey. A total of 25 responses from the sample population were dropped because the respondents were believed to have given unreliable and inconsistent answers. In all 315 questionnaires were found suitable for the analysis.

A total of 162 respondents representing 51.4% of the sample population were female and 48.6% were males. The average household size was found to be 5.15 with a minimum of 1 household member and a maximum of 16 household members. The data on education also revealed that 6.0% of the respondents do not have formal education while 31.4% have basic education. The majority (32.7%) of the respondents were found to have secondary level education and those who have tertiary education are 29.9%. The distribution of respondent's level of education is depicted by Figure 5.1.

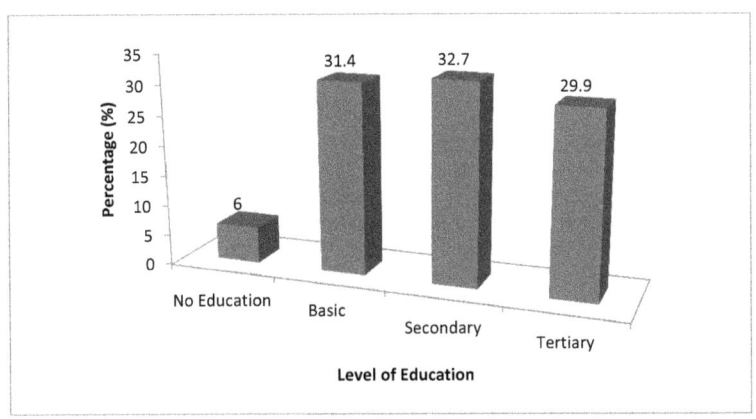

Source: Author's Survey, 2011.

Figure 5.1: Respondents Level of Education.

Concerning the age distribution of respondents, the survey revealed that 25.1% of the sample population are below the age of 29 years, 28.6% are between the ages of 30 years and 39 years, 29.5% are aged between 40 years and 49 years, 13.6% of the respondents have ages between 50 years and 59 years and a total of 3.2% are above the age of 60 years. The distribution of the age of respondents is shown in Figure 5.2.

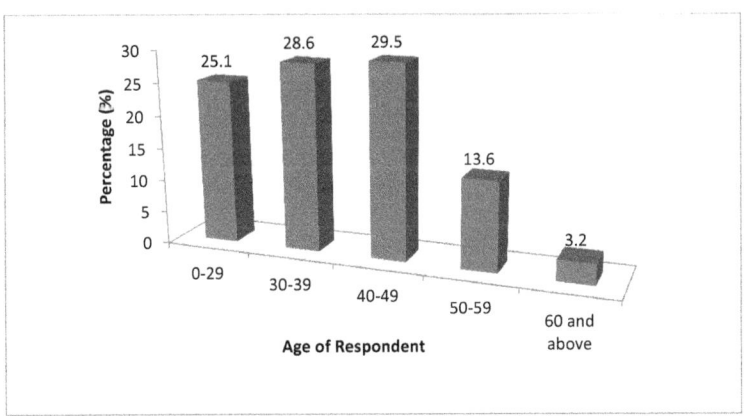

Source: Author's Survey, 2011.

Figure 5.2: Age Distribution of Respondents.

In relation to the years of stay in an area by a specific household, a minimum of 3 months up to a maximum of 50 years of stay in a particular area were observed. The average year of stay in an area was found to be 8.79 years. The marital status of respondents reveals that, 68.9% of the respondents are married while the rest are single, divorced or widowed.

Most respondents were not keen to state their earnings and others really did not know their average monthly income. Nevertheless, in an attempt to come out with a fair estimate of household's average monthly earnings, enumerators were asked to thoroughly explain to respondents that, the survey is purposely for academic purposes and that their average monthly income was not going to be used as a basis for taxation. The respondents were therefore asked to give honest responses of average monthly income. Respondents who did not know their average monthly income were asked to state their daily average income. The daily average income was then multiplied by 28 days to obtain the average monthly income. The income level of households ranges from a minimum of GH¢100 per month to a maximum of GH¢6000 per month. The average monthly income of the sample population is GH¢1001.17.

5.1.2 Respondents Ranking of Social Services

To investigate household's preferences in terms of priority, respondents were required to rank different forms of social services in accordance with their need. Six different social services were listed and these include: education, health, electricity, water, sanitation and road. The survey shows that, 41.3% of the sample population prefer Water supply as their first priority. Then comes a total of 22.9% of the sample population saying that, their first need is Health. Education, Sanitation and Electricity follow with 20.6%, 7.6% and 6.0% respectively of the sample population. Finally, a total of 1.6% of the respondents chose road as their first need. The study also revealed that, a total of 32.1% of the sample respondents prefer water supply as their second need. Figure 5.3 shows the way households ranked social services in order of importance. In the overall assessment, we can clearly conclude that respondents in the Accra-Tema metropolis rank water supply as one of their first priority social services.

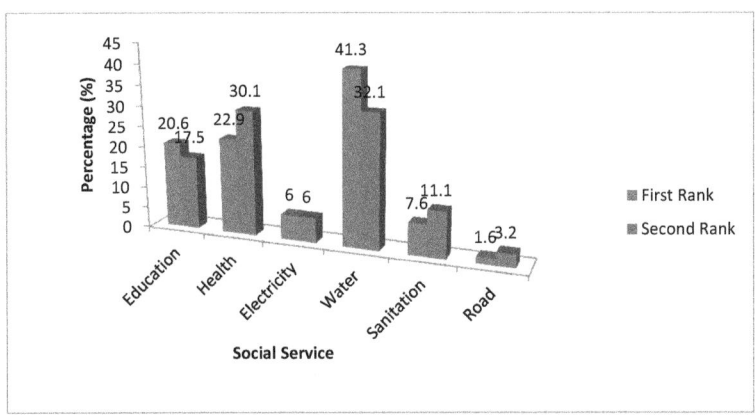

Source: Author's Survey, 2011.
Figure 5.3: Respondents ranking of Social Services.

5.1.3 Existing/Current Water Use Conditions and Problems

From the results of the survey, almost all the households interviewed (83.5%) used piped water from the GWCL as their main source of water for domestic purposes. Only 6.7% and 9.8% of households surveyed used boreholes and dug wells as their main source of water respectively. Sources of piped water in the survey area consist of private piped water, shared piped water in compound, public tabs/standpipes and tanker operators (private vendors). The results also show that 142 households representing 45.1% of the sample population have in-house piped system (private piped water and shared piped water in compound) of which a total of 63.4% have private pipe connections in their homes. The rest (36.6%) use shared piped water system in compound. Table 5.1 indicates that 19.4% of the total respondents obtain piped water purchased from tanker operators (private vendors) and 19% of the sample gets water from public tabs/standpipes. This result to some extent confirms the findings of Abraham et al. (2007) which states that, about 80% of households in the metropolis have access to potable water but only 45% have a household connection or at best a yard connection.

Table 5.1: Households Major source of water

Source of Water	Number of Households	Percentage (%)
Private Piped water	90	28.6
Shared Piped Water in Compound	52	16.5
Public tab/Standpipe	60	19.0
Tanker Operator (Private Vendor)	61	19.4
Borehole	21	6.7
Well	31	9.8
Total	315	100.0

Source: Author's Survey, 2011.

All the respondents who have in-house piped water also have alternative source of water supply. This is as a result of irregular water flow through pipes to homes in the metropolis. The maximum amount of days that respondents get water in a week is five days and the minimum is one day. The average number of days that respondents get water in a week is 3.37 days. The result of the number of days that respondents get water is shown by Table 5.2.

Table 5.2: Number of Days that water flows in a Week

Number of Days/Week	Frequency	Percentage (%)
1	14	9.9
2	26	18.3
3	27	19.0
4	43	30.3
5	32	22.5
6	---	-----
7	---	-----
Total	142	100

Source: Author's Survey, 2011.

One other concern is the number of hours that water flows in a day. Apart from the fact that water supply is not every day of the week, about 14.8% of the respondents who are using in-house water supply services reported that the number of hours that water flows to their homes is at most 4 hours in a day. Approximately 54.9% also reported that the number of hours that water flows to their homes is between 4 and 8 hours in a day. The remaining 30.3% reported that the number of hours water flows to their homes is above 8 hours in a day. The result of number of hours that water flows in a day is depicted in Table 5.3.

Table 5.3: Number of Hours that Water Flows in a Day

Number of Hours/Day	Number of Households	Percentage (%)
Less than 4hours	21	14.8
4-8hours	78	54.9
8hours and above	43	30.3
Total	142	100.0

Source: Author's Survey, 2011.

These respondents[16] also complained that, even though they have water flowing to their homes, the water flows at odd hours of the day. They argued that, sometimes the water flows during the night when everybody is asleep and sometimes during the day when nobody is in the house. These tables (Table 5.2 and Table 5.3) contradict the report by WaterAid (2005) concerning the coverage of water supply to households in the metropolis that states that 25% of the population have continuous[17] water supply. We can

---

[16] Those using in-house water supply systems.
[17] 24 hours 7 days a week supply.

therefore conclude that, though households are actually connected, the majority are using alternative sources[18] water supply.

The survey result also indicated that out of the 173 respondents who reported that they are not using in-house water supply system, 136 representing 78.6% of them reported that, they are not using the existing in-house piped water system because they don't have access, 5.8% reported that they cannot afford the price of piped water system and the rest (15.6%) reported that they are using these alternative sources (Public tabs/standpipes, tanker operators (private vendors), boreholes and dug wells) because they are more reliable than the in-house piped water system.

Households using in-house piped water system spend an average of GH¢0.127 per bucket on water from alternative sources whereas households who are not using in-house water system spend an average of GH¢0.128 per bucket on water. In general, household's average monthly water consumption is about GH¢41.14 with average per capita consumption of water being about 35.5 litres per person per day using the average household size of 5.15 persons obtained from the survey.

The survey results also indicated that, households on average spend about 38.7minutes to collect water from their existing source of water. This includes those who have in-house system but using alternative sources and those who do not have in-house piped water system.

The level of satisfaction of respondents with the existing water supply service is extremely low. Only about 22.0% of the respondents said they are satisfied with the existing service. Cross-tabulating the results confirmed that those who are dissatisfied are seeking more improved services and are more willing to pay for such service.

Unreliability of supply, poor quality and quantity of water supplied are the most serious problems associated with the current water service in the metropolis. More than half of the respondents (67.3%) reported that their source of water supply is unreliable. In addition to this, 79.7% of the respondents mentioned that the quality of water from their respective sources is not good. Most of the respondents complained that the water from their respective sources is most of the time not good for cooking let alone drinking. In all about 63.8% of the respondents reported that the quantity of water supplied to their homes is very low.

5.1.4 Existing Household Sanitation Practice

The survey result indicates that, 40% of the respondents are currently using flush toilet while about 41.3% are using pit latrine. The remaining 18.7% are users of off-site sanitation (public latrine and bush). The result also shows that, households who are using public latrine spend an average of GH¢0.51 per day on this facility. In all, approximately 45.4% of the sample is not satisfied with their current sanitation practices. Table 5.4 shows the distribution of household sanitation practices.

---

[18] Public tabs/standpipes, tanker operators (private vendors), boreholes and dug wells.

Table 5.4: Existing Household Sanitation Practice

Type of Sanitation	Existing Sanitation Technology	Number of Households	Percentage (%)
On-site	Flush toilet	126	40.0
	Pit latrine	130	41.3
Off-site	Public latrine	54	17.1
	Bush	5	1.6
	Streets	---	------
Total		315	100.0

Source: *Author's Survey, 2011.*

In the survey, five starting bid prices were used. These bids were set following what we obtained from the pilot survey. Respondents were asked to respond "yes" or "no" as to whether they will be willing to pay the initial bid price. The data revealed that 58.6% said yes to the initial price that has been given. The rest refused and gave a lower bid than the initial price.

5.2 Estimated Ordered Probit Model

As indicated earlier, in addition to the descriptive analysis, an econometric analysis may provide better information and clearer focus on the factors that affect WTP responses so that policy recommendations can be based on firm conclusions. The WTP question for the hypothetical good was presented to all respondents (both those who have access to the existing piped water system and those who have no access). The general approach of this technique is to investigate the relationship between the hypothetical determinants and the WTP responses. The variables included in the model were mainly based on the degree of their theoretical importance and their significant impact on WTP.

An important step that we must consider before the estimation is done is data exploration. To begin, we will test whether multicollinearity is present in the model or not. A simple correlation matrix was used to do this. Gujarati (1995) establishes a rule of thumb which says that, multicollinearity is a serious problem when the correlation coefficient between two variables is 0.8 or above. From the correlation matrix conveyed (Appendix A), multicollinearity does not exist in our model.

The Likelihood Ratio (LR) test statistic of the model equals 388.10 and it is $\chi^2(14)$ distributed under the null hypothesis that all the variables together have no significance influence on the WTP for improved water supply services. The critical value for this distribution with $\alpha=0.01$ is 30.58, which means that we can reject the null hypothesis. Thus, we can conclude that all the variables together do have a significant impact on the WTP for improved water supply services.

The pseudo R^2 reported is the goodness-of-fit measure and it is also known as the Likelihood Ratio Index (LRI). The likelihood ratio index (LRI) can be used to measure the goodness of fit and this value normally lies between zero and one. According to Greene (2008), the range of values has no natural interpretation but as LRI approaches one, it represents an improvement in the goodness of fit. An LRI of 0.3247 (see Appendix

B for detailed calculation) shows that, the model is adequate and it explains 32.47% of the variation. In a study by Carson and Mitchell (1989), they suggested that a contingent valuation study which fails to report an R^2 of at least 0.15, using key variables, is open to question about its reliability. An LRI of 0.3247 passes the Carson and Mitchell's proposed pseudo R^2 criterion.

The ordered probit model successfully identified many significant variables associated with the WTP for improved water system services. The estimates of the ordered probit model using STATA (version 11) are presented in Table 5.5.

Table 5.5: Ordered Probit estimate of determinants of WTP for improved water supply services

Variable (X)	Coefficient (β)	Std. Error	β/Std. Error	P>|z|	Mean of X
INC	0.00075***	0.00012	6.25	0.000	1001.17
ECW	0.00150	0.00374	0.40	0.689	41.14
TSWS	0.00662**	0.00303	2.18	0.029	38.71
HSIZ	-0.02140	0.03192	0.67	0.503	5.15
SEX	0.24914*	0.14043	1.77	0.076	0.51
BEDU	0.24942	0.28403	0.86	0.380	0.31
SEDU	0.59851**	0.28896	2.07	0.038	0.33
TEDU	1.20888***	0.34086	3.55	0.000	0.298
YRSA	0.01114	0.00811	1.37	0.169	8.79
PQEW	-0.45227**	0.17892	2.53	0.011	0.20
REL	0.19686	0.16095	1.22	0.221	0.32
IB	-1.72753	4.47438	0.39	0.699	0.098
SATN	1.06870***	0.16223	6.59	0.000	0.40
MSR	0.75820***	0.14729	5.14	0.000	0.69
cut1	0.70018				
cut2	2.04689				
cut3	3.33943				
cut4	4.76036				
	Log-Likelihood	-334.66194			
	LR $\chi^2(14)$	321.80			
	Pseudo R^2	0.3247			
***Significant at 1%, **Significant at 5%, *Significant at 10%					

All the variables in the model have the expected signs but not all of them are statistically significant. The following variables were not significant even at 10% significant level: Existing or Current Cost of Water; Number of Individuals in the Household; Reliability of Existing Water Supply Source; Respondents' Years of stay in the Area; and Initial Bid. This implies that statistically they do not influence the WTP for improved water supply in the metropolis.

The variable household income is highly significant at 1% level of significant and is positively related to the WTP for improved water supply services. This is consistent with economic theory which says demand is positively related to income in the case of normal goods. This result to some extent contradicts the findings of Jordan and Elgnaheeb (1993), Aguillar and Sterner (1995), Adjei (1999) who reported that income have a positive impact on WTP for improved water supply services but is statistically insignificant. However, Whittington et al. (1991) and Fissha (2006) reported that income significantly influence the WTP for improved water supply services.

The other highly significant variable at 1% significant level is the marital status of the respondent. As expected, it has a positive sign which indicates that married people are more cautious of the health and other risks associated with poor water supply service due to family responsibility than their single, divorced and widowed counterparts. This is consistent with the findings of Fissha (2006) using the probit econometric model and contradicts the findings of Fissha (2006) who reported that marital status of the respondent have a negative statistically insignificant impact on the willingness to pay for improved water supply services in the tobit econometric model.

Sanitation facility used by household is also highly significant at 1% significant level. As also expected, households who are using better quality sanitation facility (flush toilet) are more likely to pay more for improved water supply services than those who are using pit latrines and off-site sanitation facilities. This is mainly due to the problems associated with the use of flush toilet when there is no water. This outcome is also consistent with the findings of Fissha (2006).

Another variable that is significant is the household's perceived quality of existing water. This variable is found to be significant at 5% and as also expected has a negative sign. This indicates that households who perceive the quality of existing supply as low are likely to pay more for improved water supply services than households who perceive better water quality. This result is in line with the findings of Whittington et al. (1991), World Bank (1993), Adjei (1999) and Fissha (2006).

The time that the household spend to fetch water from current source is also statistically significant at 5%. This variable has the expected positive sign. This implies that, the more time a household spends in collecting water, the more time is wasted in doing other productive activities. Therefore households who spend more time in fetching water are likely to pay more for improved water supply services. This outcome is consistent with the findings of the World Bank (1993) but contradicts the findings of Appau-Danso (2004) who obtained a negative sign and argued that, the negative relationship may be as a result of the fact that, respondents are not directly involved in the collection of water.

Sex of the respondent is also significant at 10%. This implies that men are more likely to pay for an improved water supply than women. This may be due to the fact that women in general do not have equal control over or access to household's financial resources. This to some extent confirms the result of the World Bank (1993) that says that the impact of gender is strongly dependent on the specific cultural context.

Respondent's level of education has the expected positive sign. Tertiary education and secondary education are statistically significant at 1% and 5% respectively but primary education is not statistically significant 10%. The magnitude of the coefficients (0.27051 for Basic; 0.56093 for Secondary; and 1.19272 for Tertiary) indicates that respondents with higher level of education (or increased level of education) will be much more aware of the health benefits of improved water supply services and are therefore more likely to pay for improved water services. It can also be attributed to the fact that educated households might for a variety of reasons have higher opportunity costs for time spent in collecting water from sources outside their homes and sickness caused by poor quality water supplied and therefore will be more likely to pay for improved water supply service.

This finding is consistent with the findings of Bah (1992), Jordan and Elgnaheeb (1993), World Bank (1993), Appau-Danso (2004) and Noor and Siddiqi (2009). This shows that, the level of education of an individual is very important in determining his/her probability of willing to pay for an improved water supply system. Thus willingness to pay is much more influenced by the knowledge that individuals have on the risk associated with using poor quality water.

The initial bid which is used to test for the existence of starting point bias has a negative sign. The negative sign implies that respondents' WTP amount is downwards biased. However, in this study initial bid is found to be statistically insignificant. This phenomenon partly reflects the efficiency of using the discrete choice with follow-up elicitation format than discrete choice and iterative bidding formats which mostly leads to starting point bias.

The negative relationship between household size and WTP for improved water supply services is consistent with the findings of Aguillar and Sterner (1995) but contradicts the findings of Appau-Danso (2004). In both cases the household size significantly influence WTP but it is not statistically significant in this study. Again respondents' years of stay in an area has the expected positive sign which is consistent with the findings of Bah (1997) but it is not statistically significant. The current cost of water has the expected positive sign but it is not consistent with the findings of Olajujigbe and Fasakin (2010) which was statistically significant.

It is argued that, the coefficients of the ordered probit model cannot be interpreted directly and it is quite unclear how these coefficients should be interpreted. A positive sign however, tells whether the choice probabilities shift to higher categories when the explanatory variable increases (Greene, 2008).

Marginal effects of changes in the regressors are found by evaluating the partial derivatives of the probabilities of each outcome of the dependent variable with respect to the regressor of interest. It is also important to note that the marginal effects for a given variable in Table 5.6 sums up to zero, with negative signs showing the WTP categories where the probabilities fall and the positive signs showing the WTP categories where the probabilities rise. The marginal effects therefore show the relative changes in probabilities for a one unit change in a particular explanatory variable. This is not so for dummy variables. The marginal effect of a dummy variable is the change in the predicted probability for a change in the variable from the start value to the end value (for example, a change from 0 to 1) holding all other variables at their sample mean (Long, 1997).

As stated earlier, the variables that significantly discriminate among the various categories of WTP amount that individuals will be willing to pay are household income, time spent to fetch water from current access point, sex, education level (secondary and tertiary education to be precise), perceived quality of existing water supplied, sanitation facility of household and marital status of respondent. Table 5.6 shows the impact on the amount people are willing to pay as the levels or values of these explanatory variables change in the future.

Table 5.6: Estimated marginal effects of the Ordered Probit Model

Variable	P(WTP≤4GHp)	P(4GHp<WTP≤8GHp)	P(8GHp<WTP≤12GHp)	P(12GHp<WTP≤16GHp)	P(WTP>16GHp)
INC	-0.00005	-0.00021	0.00004	0.00019	0.00003
ECW	-0.00010	-0.00042	0.00008	0.00039	0.00005
TSWS	-0.00046	-0.00184	0.00034	0.00172	0.00024
HSIZ	0.00149	0.00596	-0.00111	-0.00557	-0.00077
SEX	-0.01757	-0.06916	0.01315	0.06455	0.00902
PEDU	-0.01602	-0.06851	0.00807	0.06639	0.01006
SEDU	-0.03561	-0.15896	0.00501	0.16122	0.02834
TEDU	-0.06249	-0.28815	-0.05130	0.31773	0.08422
YRSA	-0.00078	-0.00310	0.00058	0.00290	0.00040
PQEW	0.04078	0.12538	-0.04653	-0.10710	-0.01250
REL	-0.01291	-0.05431	0.00738	0.5213	0.00771
IB	0.12025	0.48117	-0.08929	-0.44970	-0.06243
SATN	-0.06873	-0.27126	0.00691	0.27696	0.05612
MSR	-0.07143	-0.20444	0.07747	0.17647	0.02193

The results confirm that, in general, as people's income increases, they would be willing to pay higher for improved water supply services. However, as argued by Wedgewood et al. (2003), the price elasticity of demand is very low. From the result, as household income increases by 10%, there is only a 0.03% chance that households would be willing to pay an amount greater than GH¢0.16 per bucket and a 0.2% chance that households would be willing to pay an amount greater than GH¢0.12 but less or equal to GH¢0.16.

Also, as the time that households spend to fetch water from current access point increases, they would be willing to pay higher amounts. A 10% increase in the time has only 1.7 percentage chance of making households pay an amount greater than GH¢0.12 but less or equal to GH¢0.16. The results also shows that, there is 0.2% chance that an increase of 10% in the time spent to fetch water from existing access point would make the respondent willing to pay an amount greater than GH¢0.16.

The result shows that the probability of paying an amount for improved water supply system is higher for men than women. From Table 5.6, we can observe that the probability of paying an amount above GH¢0.16 is 0.009 higher for men than women. This contradicts the results of Whittington et al. (1991), Jordan and Elgnaheeb (1993), Aguillar and Sterner (1995) in Limon, Costa Rica who reported that the probability of paying for improved water supply is lower for men than women and confirms the result of Aguillar and Sterner (1995) in Muag Xiathani, Laos who reported that male respondents have higher WTP for improved water supply than females. This outcome also confirms the World Bank (1993) claim that the impact of gender on WTP for improved water strongly depends on the specific cultural context.

The level of education also relates positively with the probability of the individual's willingness to pay for improved water supply system. The result suggests that highly educated individuals have a higher probability of WTP for improved services. The probability of paying an amount greater than GH¢0.12 but less than or equal to GH¢0.16 is 0.16 (0.317 - 0.161) higher for tertiary educated individuals than secondary educated individuals. There is also a 0.25 (0.317-0.066) chance that tertiary educated individuals would pay an amount greater than GH¢0.12 but less than or equal to GH¢0.16 for improved water supply services than individuals who have only primary education. The results also indicated that, respondents who have tertiary education have a higher probability of 0.32 for paying a higher amount which is greater than GH¢0.12 but less than or equal to GH¢0.16 than individual who have no education.

The perceived quality of existing water is negatively related to the WTP for improved water supply. As shown by the result, the probability of paying a higher amount which is above GH¢0.16 is 0.013 lower for respondents who perceive the quality of existing water supplied as high than households who perceive the quality to be low.

Based on the results from the computation of marginal effects, there is a 0.056 chance that households using better quality sanitation facility (flush toilet) will pay an amount which is above GH¢0.16 for improved water supply services than households who use pit latrine and public toilet. The results also indicated that, respondents who are married have a higher probability of 0.022 for paying a higher amount which is greater than GH¢0.16 than respondents who are single, divorced or widowed.

5.3   Total Willingness to Pay and Total Revenue

In analysing the Maximum Willingness to pay (MWTP) estimate from the open ended question, it was revealed that the mean WTP for improved water supply services is GH¢0.10 per bucket. This implies that on average, households are willing to pay an amount of GH¢0.10 per bucket for improved water supply services. This further implies that on the average households are willing to pay approximately seven times higher than the current price[19] that households using water from GWCL pay per bucket. Inadvertently the mean, median and modal WTP was GH¢0.10 per bucket.

Table 5.7: Analysis of Maximum WTP reported from the open ended question

Variable	Obs	Mean	Mode	Median	Std. Dev.	Minimum	Maximum
WTP	315	0.1000635	0.10	0.10	.0545129	.02	.20
		*Mean WTP= GH¢0.10, Minimum= GH¢0.02 and Maximum=GH¢0.20					

Source: Author's Survey, 2011.

---

[19] The GWCL charges GHp80 per 1000 litres (55 buckets) of water which is about GHp1.45 per bucket.

In the next paragraph we estimate the Total WTP and the economic cost of inadequate and poor water supplied to the metropolis. The estimation of the total WTP and therefore the cost of inadequate and poor water supply are made possible by extrapolating the results from the sample to the population.

According to the Ghana Statistical Service report[20] on the 2010 population and housing census, the population of the Accra-Tema metropolis is 4,192,370 (Accra's population is 3,963,264 and that of Tema is 229,106). According to International Food Policy Research Institute's (IFPRI) report in 2003, the average household size of Accra-Tema metropolis stood at 5.1 persons per household. Dividing the population by the average household size and after rounding to the nearest whole number, we found out that there are 822,033 households in the Accra-Tema metropolis. According to WHO (2005), the average water requirement for each person is 70 litres (approximately 4 buckets) per person per day. Based on the average household size of 5.1 persons per household, each household is supposed to use a total of 346.8 litres (approximately 20.4 buckets) of water per day. This means that the entire population in the Accra-Tema metropolis is supposed to use a total of 285,081,044.4 litres (approximately 16,769,473 buckets) of water per day.

The concept of valuing the economic cost of inadequate and poor water supply in the metropolis is attributed to the total amount that households are willing to pay for improvement in the water supply system in the metropolis. In other words, the total amount that households are willing to pay at the margin is equal to the cost of inadequate and poor water supply in the metropolis.

Estimating the total WTP is made possible by extrapolating the results of the sample to the population. As a result the mean WTP from the survey is used as the population mean. This reflects the average amount that households are prepared to pay per bucket for improvement in the water supply system. The choice of the population mean over the sample mean is necessary because it would make it possible for us to extrapolate the results for the entire population.

Thus the total willingness to pay for the entire population is given by;

$$TWTP = (mWTP) \times N$$

Where TWTP = Total Willingness to pay

mWTP = population mean Willingness to pay per bucket

N = Total number of buckets of water consumed by total number of households in the metropolis per day.

From the survey, the mean WTP is GH¢0.10 per bucket. This implies that on the average households in the metropolis are willing to pay GH¢0.10 per bucket for improvement in the water supply system in the metropolis. As indicated earlier, the amount of water

---

[20] http://en.wikipedia.org/wiki/Ghana

Source: Author's Survey, 2011

required to be consumed per day by the entire households in the metropolis is approximately equal to 16,769,473 buckets.

Thus the estimated total WTP for improved water supply is expressed as;

$$TWTP = GHp10 \; x \; 16,769,473$$

$$TWTP = GHp167,694,730.00$$

$$TWTP = GH¢1,676,947.30$$

Therefore the economic cost of inadequate and poor water supply in the metropolis is estimated to be about GH¢1,676,947.30 per day. This clearly shows that indeed inadequate and poor water supplied to the metropolis imposes a huge economic burden on the metropolis, the country and therefore adversely affects the welfare of its citizens.

In the next few paragraphs, we also estimate the Total WTP and Total Revenue at various prices for a bucket of water. The estimation of the total WTP and the total revenue is also made possible by extrapolating the results from the sample to the population.

Table 5.8: Total WTP and Total Revenue for Improved Water Service (pesewas per bucket)

WTP interval (GHp)	Mid WTP (GHp)	Freq. Dist.		Share of Population	Cumulative Population	Total No. of buckets used per day	Total WTP per day (GHp)
		No. of HH[21]	Percentage (%)				
A	B	C	D	$E_i=D_i*822,033$	$F_i=E_i+E_{i-1}$	$G_i=F_i*20.4$[22]	$J_i=B_i*G_i$
16.1—20	18.05	42	13.3	109,330	109,330	2,230,332.0	40,257,492.60
12.1—16	14.05	62	19.7	161,941	271,271	5,533,928.4	77,751,694.02
8.1—12	10.05	75	23.8	195,644	466,915	9,525,066.0	**95,726,913.30**
4.1—8	6.05	88	28.0	230,169	697,084	14,220,513.6	86,034,107.28
0—4	**2.00**	48	15.2	124,949	822,033	16,769,473.2	**33,538,946.40**
Total		315	100.0	822,033			

Source: Author's Survey, 2011.

Table 5.8 shows that charging an amount of GH¢0.10 per bucket results in a higher total revenue of GH¢957,269.13 per day. However, from the table, majority of the population would be able to pay GH¢0.02 per bucket which would yield the lowest expected revenue of GH¢335,389.46 per day. The choice of price per bucket of water set by the service provider would ultimately depend on the objective of the policy. If the objective of the provider is not necessarily to maximise revenue but however to ensure maximisation of water coverage so as to ensure a substantial reduction in the problems of water supply in the metropolis, then the provider would set the price at GH¢0.02 per bucket. On the other hand if the objective of the policy is to maximise profit, then the optimal price would be set at GH¢0.10 per bucket.

---

[21] HH implies Households
[22] The average household water consumption per day.

We also estimate the demand curve for the proposed improved water supply service in terms of the total number of households and their associated MWTP. Household's demand for water and expected total revenue is shown in Table 5.8 and the demand curve (obtained by regressing Cumulative Population on the Mid WTP) is represented by Figure 5.4.

The downward slope of the demand curve indicates that improved water supply services in the Accra-Tema metropolis is a normal good.

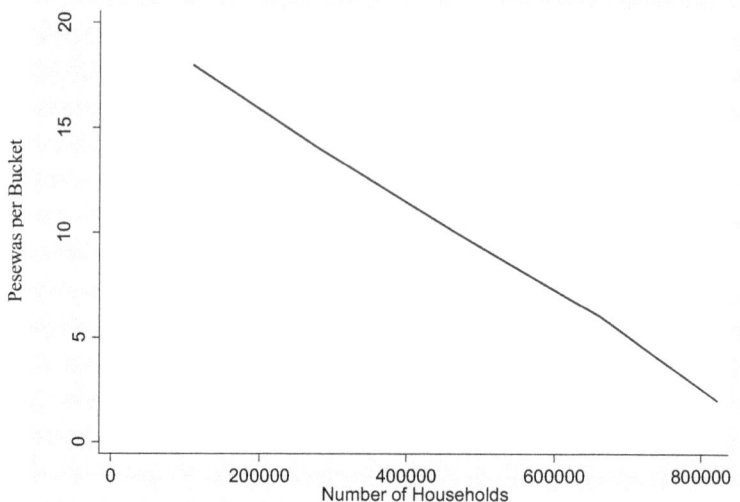

Source: Author's Survey, 2011.

Figure 5.4: Household's Demand for Water.

The estimated household demand curve was used to estimate consumers' surplus and total revenue at different tariff rates. From the survey results, the proportion of respondents who use in-house piped water (private piped water and shared piped water in compound) accounted for 45% of the sample population. This implies that, approximately a total of 369,915 households of the total number of households use these sources.

Figure 5.5 shows the possible consumer surplus and revenue that would be obtained if the service authority improves the water supply service, charges the existing tariff rate (GHp1.45 per bucket) and the coverage remain unchanged. At the current tariff level of GHp1.45 per bucket, all the households in the metropolis will go for the improved water supply service and therefore the consumer surplus and expected total revenue that would accrue to households and the service provider if each household consume one bucket of water are represented by trapezoid CHGA and rectangle EIHC respectively. Thus the possible consumer surplus and total revenue per day (which is calculated by multiplying the average household water consumption of 20.4 buckets by the areas of the trapezoid CHGA and rectangle EIHC) would be GH¢1,246,731.35 and GH¢210,817.54 respectively (see Appendix F *(i)* for detailed calculation).

However, due to supply constraints (insufficient funds and infrastructure) only 369,915 households representing 45% of the total number of households in the metropolis would be covered and thus the consumer surplus and expected total revenue that would accrue to households and the service provider if each household consume one bucket of water are represented by trapezoid CDBA and rectangle EFDC respectively. The possible consumer surplus and expected total revenue that would be obtained per day (which is calculated by multiplying the average household water consumption of 20.4 buckets by the areas of the trapezoid CDBA and rectangle EFDC) are GH¢728,814.55 and GH¢77,081.04 respectively (see Appendix F *(ii)* for details of the calculation).

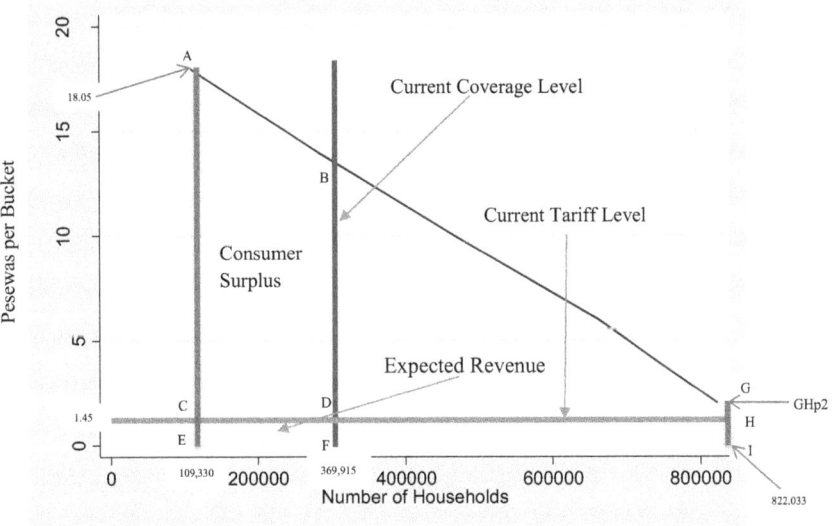

Figure 5.5: Revenue and consumers' surplus from charging the current tariff level.

Moreover, as illustrated in Figure 5.6, if the tariff rate for the improved water is set at GH¢0.05 per bucket (which is half of the mean WTP) with supply being assured through new investment, our estimation suggests that the number of households who would be able to pay GH¢0.05 per bucket would be approximately 708,019 households. This will result in an increase in the total revenue from GH¢77,081.04 to GH¢610,662.78 and consumer surplus from GH¢728,814.55 to GH¢796,914.93 (see Appendix F *(iii)* for details of the calculation). The possible consumer surplus and expected total revenue that would be obtained if each household consume one bucket of water are represented by triangle JKL and rectangle MNKJ respectively in Figure 5.6.

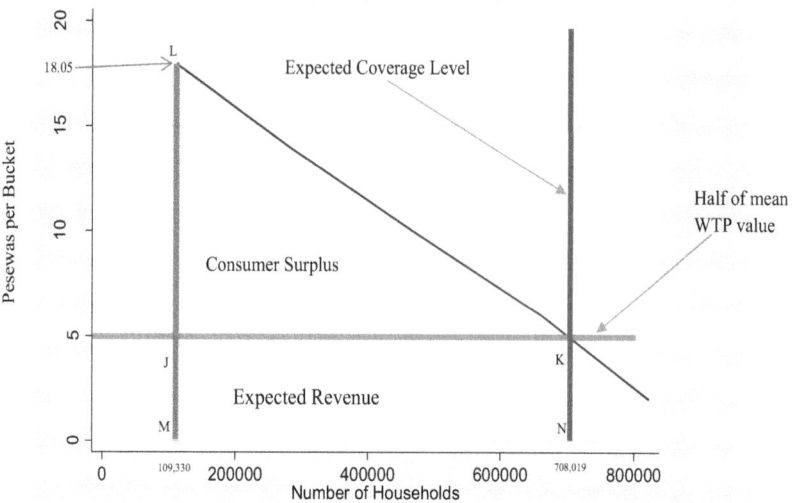

Figure 5.6: Expected Revenue and consumers' surplus from charging half of mean WTP.

The situation will change if the tariff level is set at the mean WTP (at GH¢0.10 per bucket) derived from the survey with supply being assured through new investment. The estimation suggests that the number of households who would be able to afford GH¢0.10 per bucket would be 475,460 households. This means that the number of households being covered will decrease compared to the situation where the price is set at GH¢0.05 (half of mean WTP) per bucket (708,019 households) but the coverage level will not fall below the current coverage level (369,915 households). The possible consumer surplus per day will decrease substantially from GH¢796,914.93 to GH¢300,629.34 and expected total revenue will increase from GH¢610,622.78 to GH¢746,905.20 (see Appendix F *(iv)* for details of the calculation). The possible consumer surplus and expected total revenue that would be obtained if each household consume one bucket of water are represented by triangle PQR and rectangle STQP respectively in Figure 5.7. As shown in Figure 5.7, consumer surplus will fall considerably but total revenue will increase.

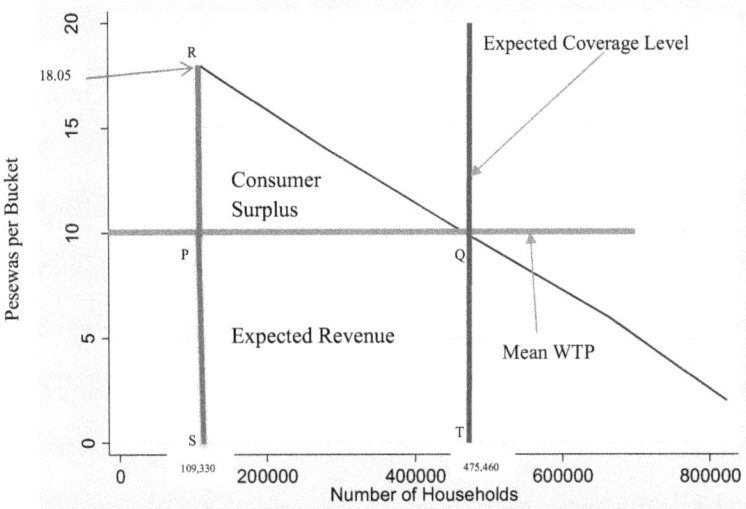

Figure 5.7: Expected Revenue and consumers' surplus from charging the Mean WTP.

In a nut shell, the results of this study show that the tariff for improved water can be increased substantially with unconstrained supply before an insignificant number of households would be covered under the proposed improved water supply system. Results from our analysis further indicated that, households in the Accra-Tema metropolis are prepared to pay on the average about GH¢0.10 for a bucket of water which is about 7 times more than what they are paying currently. Therefore, policy recommendation emanating from the study is that, government should improve on water infrastructure and consequently water supply and increase tariffs since people are prepared to pay more for improved water supply.

CHAPTER SIX

CONCLUSION AND RECOMMENDATIONS

This chapter concludes the work and looks at the policy recommendations based on the results. The chapter also makes possible suggestion for future research.

6.1 Conclusion

Most of the challenges facing many developing countries in the world today in their struggle for economic and social development are increasingly related to water. The urban water sector in most of these nations is faced with serious constraints in meeting the challenge to provide potable water for all urban residents. This is due to insufficient structures and funds coupled with rapid population growth and urbanisation.

As supply side problems are in fact eminent, demand side issues have revealed much significance. Inadequate knowledge about people's preferences and WTP for public services has been a major obstacle. In other words, as supply side features seems to be overdone, there is only a little that is being done in the demand side. Therefore this study is intended to bridge the information gap for policy initiatives.

In an attempt to investigate how consumers are willing to pay for improved water supply services, this study has shed some light on the current condition of the provision of potable water in the Accra-Tema metropolis. The study has shown that the provision of potable water in the metropolis is unreliable, it is of poor quality and the quantity supplied to households is woefully inadequate. It has also been observed that UfW which accounts for about 60% of total production is most of the time as a result of leakages of transmission lines from treatment plants to customers. Unmetered customers as well as illegal removal of water for agricultural purposes are also causes of UfW.

The study aims to analyse household's valuation of improved water supply services in the Accra-Tema metropolis. A contingent valuation survey was conducted to obtain data from a sample of 315 households. The elicitation format used was the discrete choice with a follow-up approach and the survey was administered using in-person interview. We also used both descriptive and econometric analytical technique. The ordered probit econometric model was used to analyse the determinants of household's WTP for improved water supply services.

The descriptive analysis shows that only 45% of the respondents reported that they do have in-house piped water system. About 68% of the respondents reported that their existing water source is unreliable, about 64% of the respondents reported that the quantity of water supply is very low. In all, about 80% of the respondents stated that the quality of water supplied to their homes is poor. This implies that the main problems of existing water supply service in the metropolis are unreliability of supply, poor quality and quantity of water supply. Results from the demand and supply analysis suggest that consumers are prepared to pay more for improved water supply services. On the average, consumers are prepared to pay about 7 times what is being charged currently. Specifically, consumers are prepared to pay on average GH¢0.10 for a bucket of water.

An econometric analysis using ordered probit model was also carried out to investigate the relationship between WTP responses and the hypothetical determinants. In summary, there were fourteen explanatory variables included in the regression model based on their theoretical importance and their significant impact on WTP for improved water supply services. In general, all the signs of the coefficients of the explanatory variables are in the expected direction. Income, time spent to fetch water from existing source, sex, secondary level of education, tertiary level of education, perceived quality of current water supply, sanitation facility and marital status have a significant impact on WTP. The variable initial bid has a negative and insignificant effect on the probability of saying yes to the proposed bid. This implies that the study is free from starting point bias.

In a nut shell, the overall assessment of the study demonstrates that the WTP responses from the contingent valuation survey using the discrete choice with a follow-up elicitation format are not ad hoc but they are systematically related to the explanatory variables suggested by theory. Hence, it is possible to suggest the contingent valuation method as a feasible method for estimating the WTP for improved water supply services.

6.2   Recommendations

Based on the findings, we can draw the following policy recommendations:

- The findings of the study shown that there is a strong positive relationship between sanitation facility and WTP for improved water supply services. This implies that improving sanitation service cannot be done without improvements in water supply. Therefore improvement in better sanitation service should be adequately secured so that people will be more willing to pay for effective and efficient improvement in water supply services since availability of water supply compliments better sanitation facilities.

- The study also showed that there is a strong relationship between the level of education and the WTP for improved water supply services. An important policy recommendation that can be derived from this relationship is that, the service provider should make use of price discrimination technique to charge highly educated people higher prices than people who have low level of education since highly educated people are more willing to pay for improved water supply services than people who have low levels of education.

- We also found out from the study that the revenue that the service provider receives from its production is below cost recovery levels because of the high rate of UfW (which is about 60% of total production). The service provider can therefore increase its revenue and also reduce the acute water supply in the metropolis by taking measures to reduce the rate of UfW in the metropolis. It also emerged from the study that supply cannot satisfy the existing demand and this has led to a situation whereby households are forced to acquire water from secondary sources where they pay a price that is about nine[23] times more than the approved price per bucket. They are also force to waste a considerable amount of

---

[23] On average households spend about GHp12.75 per bucket on water

time in fetching water from these secondary sources. The service provider can increase its total revenue by improving the water supply system and increasing tariff since households are willing to pay more than the existing tariff.

- Moreover, the revenue from increased tariffs should be used as an investment fund which will give the service provider the financial capacity to deal with the acute water supply shortage in the metropolis, which threatens to become a major problem in the country in the coming years. Furthermore, the government should focus on improving water infrastructure which will consequently help improve water supply and increase tariffs since people are prepared to pay more for improved water supply.

- Finally, the study did not consider the effective ways of reducing UfW which is one of the main causes of acute water supply shortage in the metropolis. Future research can be done on how the GWCL can effectively reduce the rate of UfW in order to reduce the acute water supply problem in the metropolis.

REFERENCES

Abraham, E. T., van Rooijen, D., Cofie, O. and Raschid-Sally, L. (2007), "Planning urban water-dependent livelihood opportunities for the poor in Accra, Ghana", SWITCH Scientific Meeting, International Water Management Institute, Accra, Ghana.

Adepoju, A. A. and Omonona, B. T. (2009), "Determinants of Willingness to Pay for Improved Water Supply in Osogbo Metropolis; Osun State, Nigeria", *Research Journal of Social Sciences*, Vol. 4, pp. 1-6.

Adjei, P.O. (1999), "Willingness to pay for improved Water Services: Contingent Valuation Method for Greater Accra Metropolitan Area", *An Unpublished MPhil Thesis*, University of Ghana.

Afroz, R., Hassan, M. N., Awang, M. and Ibrahim, N. A. (2005), "Willingness to pay for Air Quality Improvement in Klang Valley, Malaysia", *American Journal of Environmental Sciences* Vol. 1, No. 3, pp. 194-201.

Aguilar, M. and Sterner, T. (1995), "Willingness to pay for improved communal water services", EEU working papers, Gothenburg University, Sweden.

Anderson, F.R. (1993), "Natural Resource Damages, Superfund, and the Courts". In Kopp, R. J. and Smith, V. K. (eds.), "Valuing Natural Assets. The Economics of Natural Resource Damage Assessment", Washington D.C.: Resources for the Future, pp. 26-62.

Appau-Danso, E. (2004), "Willingness to pay for improved Water Supplies in Rural Communities. A case study of the Asante Akim South District", *An Unpublished MPhil Thesis*, University of Ghana.

Arrow, K. Solow, R., Portney, P., Leamer, E., Radner, R., and Schuman, H. (1993), "Report of the NOAA panel on contingent valuation". *Federal Register*, Vol. 58, No 10, pp. 4601-4614.

Asafo-Adjaye, J. and Dzator, J. (2003), "Willingness to Pay for Malaria Insurance: A case study of Households in Ghana using the Contingent Valuation Method", *Economic Analysis and Policy*, Vol. 33, No. 1, pp. 31-47.

Asfaw, A., Gustafsson-Wright, E. and van der Gaag, J. (2008), "Willingness to pay for Health Insurance: An Analysis of Potential Market for New Low Cost Health Insurance Products in Namibia", AIID RS 08-01/2.

Asenso-Okyere, W. K., Osei-Akoto, I. and Appiah, E. N. (1997), "Willingness to pay for Health Insurance in a developing economy. A pilot study of the informal sector of Ghana using contingent valuation", *Health Policy*, Vol. 42, pp. 223-237.

Awuah, E., and Assan D. (2007), "State of Water Supply in Accra".

Bah. I. (1997), "Estimating household's valuation for improved water supply service in urban areas: The case of Freetown, Sierra Leone", *Unpublished MA Dissertation*, University of Botswana.

Barbier, E.B. (1998), "Environmental Project Evaluation in Developing Countries: Valuing the Environment as Input", Note di Lavoro (86.98), Fondazione Eni E. Mattei, Milan.

Benneh, G., Songsore, J., Nabila, J. S., Amuzu, A.T., Tutu, K.A., Yangyuoru, Y. and McGranahan, G. (1993), "Environmental Problems and the Urban Household in the Greater Accra Metropolitan Area (GAMA), Ghana", Stockholm Environmental Institute.

Bishop, R. C. and Heberlein T. A. (1979), "Measuring values of extra-market goods: Are indirect measures biased?", *American Journal of Agricultural Economics*, Vol. 61, No. 5, pp. 926-930.

Bishop, R. C., Heberlein, T. A. and Kealy, M. J. (1983), "Contingent valuation of environmental assets: comparisons with a simulated market", *Natural Resources Journal*, Vol. 23, pp. 619-634.

Boadu, F.O. (1992), "Contingent Valuation for household water in rural Ghana", *Journal of American Economics*, Vol. 43, No. 3, pp. 548-465.

Boardman, A. E., Greenberg, D. H., Vining, A. R. and Weimer, D. L. (1996), "Cost-Benefit Analysis: Concept and Practice", New Jersey: A. Simon & Schuster Company.

de Boer, B., Bosch, P. R., Brouwer, R. and Duijnhouwer, F. (1997), "Monetarisering van Milieuverliezen; Eindrapport van het informele discussieplatform Monetarisering van Milieuverliezen", Centraal Bureau voor de Statistiek, Voorburg.

Bolt, K., Ruta, G. and Sarraf, M. (2005), "Estimating the Cost of Environmental Degradation", The World Bank Environment Department.
Boyle, K., Bishop, R. and Welsh, M. (1986), "Starting Point Bias in Contingent Valuation Surveys", *Land Economics,* Vol. 61, pp. 188-194.

Brookshire, D., Ives, B., and Schulze, W, (1976), "The Valuation of Aesthetic Preferences", *Journal of Environmental Economics and Management*, Vol. 3, No. 4, pp. 325-346.

Brookshire, D.S., and Whittington, D. (1993), "Water-Resources Issues in the Developing-Countries", *Water Resources Research*, Vol. 29, No. 7, pp. 1883-1888.

Brown, M.M. (2003), "Clean water-An agent of change", *Choices*, Vol. 12, No.1, pp.3-4.

Calkins, P., Larue, B. and Vézina, M. (2002), "Willingness to Pay for Drinking Water in the Sahara: The Case of Douentza in Mali", Cahiers d'économie et sociologie rurales, No. 64.

Cameron, A.C., and Trivedi, P.K. (2005), *Microeconometrics-Methods and Applications*, New York: Cambridge University Press.

Carson R. T., and Mitchell, R. C. (1981), "An Experiment in Determining Willingness to Pay for National Water Quality Improvements, draft report to the US Environmental Protection Agency", Washington DC.

Carson R. T., and Mitchell, R. C. (1984), "A Contingent Valuation Estimate of National Freshwater Benefits: Technical Report to the US Environmental Protection Agency", Resources for the Future, Washington, D.C.

Carson R. T., and Mitchell, R. C. (1989), "Using surveys to value public goods: the contingent valuation method", Resources for the Future, Washington, D.C.

Carson, R.T., and Mitchell, R.C. (1993), "Using surveys to value public goods: The Contingent Valuation Method", Resources for the Future, Washington, D.C.

Clawson, M. and Knetsch, J. (1966), *Economics of Outdoor Recreation,* Baltimore: John Hopkins University Press.

Community Water and Sanitation Agency (2004), "Strategic Investment Plan 2005 – 2015: CWSA, Accra, Ghana". http://www.cwsagh.org/documents/SIP_2005-2015.pdf

Coyne, A. and Adamowicz, W. (1992) "Modeling Choice of Site for Hunting Bighorn Sheep", *Wildlife Society Bulletin,* Vol. 20, pp. 26-33.

Cummings, R. G., Schulze W. D., Gerking, S. D., and Brookshire, D. S. (1986), "Measuring the elasticity of substitution of wages for municipal infrastructure: A comparison of the survey and wage hedonic approaches", *Journal of Environmental Economics and Management,* Vol. 13 No. 3, pp. 269-276.

Davis, R. (1963), "Recreation Planning as an Economic Problem", *Natural Resources Journal,* Vol. 3, No. 2, pp. 239-249.

Desvousges, W. H., Smith V. K., and McGivney M. P. (1983), "A comparison of alternative approaches for estimating recreation and related benefits of water quality improvements", EPA-230-05-83-001, Washington D.C., Office of Policy Analysis, U.S. Environmental Protection Agency.

Doe, H. W. (2007), "Assessing the Challenges of Water Supply in. Urban Ghana: The case of North Teshie",(EESI Master Thesis). Stockholm: Department of Land and Water Resources Engineering, Royal Institute of Technology (KTH), pp. 32 http://www.lwr.kth.se/Publikationer/PDF_Files/LWR_EX_07_06.PDF.

Dosi, C. (2000), "Environmental Values, Valuation Methods, and Natural Disaster Damage Assessment",UN ECLAC

Dowdeswell, E. (1996), "Editorial comments on water", *Our Planet,* Vol. 8, No. 3, pp. 1.

Drakakis-Smith, D.W. (2000), *Third world cities.* Routledge, London; New York.

The Dublin Statement on Water and Sustainable Development (1992), "International Conference of Water and the Environment, Dublin, Ireland".

Duncan C. S., Khattak A. J., and Council F. M. (1998), "Applying the Ordered Probit Model to Injury Severity in Truck-Passenger Car Rear-End Collisions", *Transportation Research Record,* 1635, Paper No. 98-1237.

Engel, S., Iskandarani, M., and Usache, M. P. (2005), "Improved Water Supply in the Ghanaian Volta Basin: Who uses it and Who Participates in Community Decision Making?", IFPRI, EPT Discussion paper, No. 129.

Fissha, M. (2006), "Household Demand for improved Water Service in Urban Areas: The case of Addis Ababa, Ethiopia", *Unpublished MSc. Thesis*, Addis Ababa University.

Freeman, III, A. M. (1979), *The Benefits of Environmental Improvement: Theory and Practice*, Baltimore: The Johns University Press for Resources for the Future, Inc.

Frick, K. D., Lynch, M., West, S., Munoz, B., and Mkocha, H. A. (2003), "Household Willingness to pay for Azithromycin treatment for trachoma control in the United Republic of Tanzania", *Bulletin of Word Health Organisation*, Vol. 81, pp. 101-107.

Garrod, G. D. and Willis, K. G. (1999), *Economic Valuation of the Environment*, Edward Elgar Publishing Ltd., Cheltenham, UK.

Greene, W.H. (2008), *Econometrics Analysis*, Sixth Edition, New Jersey: Prentice Hall.

Gujarati, D. (1995), *Basic Econometrics*, Third Edition, New York: McGraw-Hill Inc.

Gunatilake, H. (2003), "Environmental Valuation: Theory and Applications." Postgraduate Institute of Agriculture, University of Peradeniya, Sri Lanka.

Gyau-Boakye, P. (2001), "Sources of rural water supply in Ghana. International Water Resources Association", *Water International*, Vol. 26, No. 1, pp. 96-104.

Hanemann, W. M. (1991), "Willingness to pay and willingness to accept: how much can they differ?", *American Economic Review*, Vol. 81, pp. 635-647.

Hanemann, W. M. 1994. "Valuing the Environment through Contingent Valuation", *Journal of Econometric Perspectives* Vol. 81, pp. 635–647.

Hanley, N. (1988), "Using Contingent Valuation to Value Environmental Improvements", *Applied Economics,* Vol. 20, pp. 541-549.

Hanley, N., Mourato, S. and Wright, R. E. (2001) "Choice Modeling Approaches: A Superior Alternative for Environmental Valuation?" *Journal of Economic Surveys*, Vol. 15, No. 3, pp. 435-462.

Hanley, N., Shogren, J. F. and White, B. (2002), *Environmental Economics in Theory and Practice,* New York: Palgrave MacMillan.

Hammack, J. and Brown, G. (1974), *Waterfowl and Wetlands: Towards Bioeconomic Analysis,* Baltimore: John Hopkins University Press.

Hardoy, J.E., Mitlin, D., and Satterthwaite, D. (1992), *Environmental problems in Third World cities*. Earthscan, London.

Hausman, J. A., and Diamond, P. A. (1994). "Contingent Valuation: Is Some Number Better than No Number?" *Journal of Economic Perspectives* Vol. 8, No. 4, pp. 45–64.

Hensher, D., Shore, N., and Train, K. (2004), "Households' Willingness to Pay for Water Service Attributes".

Hoehn, J. and Randall, A. (1987), "A Satisfactory Benefit Cost Indicator from Contingent Valuation", *Journal of Environmental Economics and Management,* Vol. 14, No. 3, pp. 226-247.

Horowitz, J. K., McConnell, K. E. (2002) "A Review of WTA/WTP Studies", *Journal of Environmental Economics and Management,* Vol. 44, pp. 426-447.

International Food Policy Research Institute (2003), "Women and Children Getting by in Urban Accra". www.ifpri.org/sites/default/files/publications/accra.pdf

Jordan, J. L., and Elnagheeb, A. H. (1993), "Willingness to pay for improvement in drinking water quality", *Water Resources Research,* vol.29, No. 2, pp. 237-245.

Knetsch, J. L., and Sinden, J. A. (1984), "Willingness to pay and compensation demanded: experimental evidence of an unexpected disparity in measures of value", *Quarterly Journal of Economics,* Vol. 99, pp. 507-521.

Knetsch, J. (1993), "The Reference point and Measures of Welfare Change", paper to Canadian Conference on Environmental and Resource Economics, Ottawa.

Labite H., van der Steen P., and Lens P. (2008), "Analysis of Health Benefits versus Costs of Interventions in the Urban Water System in Accra, Using Quantitative Microbial Risks Assessment", *WaterMill Working Paper Series,* Vol. 14, pp. 8.

Lancaster, K.J. (1966), "A New Approach to Consumer Theory", *Journal of Urban Economics,* Vol. 74, pp. 132-157.

Lareau, T. and Rae, D. (1987), "Valuing Willingness to pay for Diesel Reduction Odours", *Southern Economics Journal,* pp.728-7742.

Long, J. S. (1997), *Regression Models for Categorical and Limited Dependent Variables. Advanced Techniques in the Social Sciences,* Vol. 7, California: SAGE Publications, Inc.

Limantol, A. M. (2009), "Impacts of Rural Water Supply Systems in Farming Communities: A case study of the Saboba-Cherereponi District", *An Unpublished MSc. Thesis,* Kwame Nkrumah University of Science and Technology, Ghana.

Maddala, G.S. (1983), *Limited-Dependent and Qualitative Variables in Econometrics,* New York: Cambridge University Press.

Mishra, S. K. (undated) "Valuation of Environmental Goods and Services: An Institutionalistic Assessment". https://www.msu.edu/user/schmid/mishra.htm

Mendelsohn, R. and Olmstead, S. (2009), "The Economic Valuation of Environmental Amenities and Disamenities: Methods and Applications", *Annual Review of Environment and Resources,* Vol. 34, pp. 325-347.

Munasinghe, M. (1990), "Managing Water Resources to Avoid Environmental Degradation: Policy Analysis and Application", World Bank.

New Delhi Declaration (1990), "United Nations Development Programme".

Nielson, P. (2004), "Realizing the dream", *Our Planet*, Vol. 14, No. 4, pp. 23-24.

Noor, J. A., and Siddiqi, W. (2009), "Estimation of Willingness to pay for Improvement in drinking water quality: a study of Wasa, Lahore", *Economics Bulletin*, Vol. 29, No. 2, pp.A19.

Organization for Economic Cooperation and Development (2007), "African Economic Outlook 2007 - Ghana Country Note".http://www.oecd.org/dataoecd/26/51/38562673.pdf

Olajuyigbe, A. E., and Fasakin, J. O. (2010), "Citizens' Willingness to Pay for Improved Sustainable Water Supply in a Medium-Sized City in South Western Nigeria", *Current Research Journal of Social Sciences*, Vol. 2, No. 2, pp. 41-50.

Pearce, D. W. and Markandya, A. (1989), *Environmental Policy Benefits: Monetary Valuation*, Organisation for Economic Co-operation and Development, Paris.

Pearce, D. W. and Turner, R. K. (1990), *Economics of Natural Resources and the Environment*, Harvester, Hemel Hempsted.

Pearce, D. W. and Barbier, E. (2000), *Blueprint for a Sustainable Economy*, London: Earthscan.

Perman, R., Ma, Y., McGilvary, J. and Common, M. (2003), *Natural Resources and Environmental Economics,* Third Edition, London: Pearson Addison Wesley.

Randall, A., Ives, B. and Eastman, C. (1974), "Bidding Games for the Valuation of Aesthetic Environmental Improvements", *Journal of Environmental Economics and Management,* Vol. 1, pp. 132-149.

Rodriguez, E., Lacaze, V., and Lupin, B. (2007), "Willingness to pay for organic food in Argentina: Evidence from a consumer survey", School of Economic and Social Sciences, Universidad Nacional de Mar del Plata, Argentina.

Rowe, R., d'Arge, R. and Brookshire, D. (1980), "An Experiment on the Economic Value of Visibility", *Journal of Environmental Economics and Management,* Vol. 7, pp. 1-19.

Russell, C. (1982), "Economic Incentives in the Management of Hazardous Waste, Columbia", *Journal of Environmental Law*, Vol. 13, pp. 254-274.

Serageldin, I. (1994), "Water supply, sanitation, and environmental sustainability : the financing challenge", World Bank, Washington, D.C.

Stynes, D.J. (1990). "A Note on Population Distributions and the Travel Cost Method, Chapter 9. In: Johnson, R.L. and Johnson, G.V. (eds.), *Economic Valuation of Natural Resources*, Westview Press, Boulder, pp. 139-149.

Thayer, M. (1981), "Contingent Valuation Techniques for Assessing Environmental Impacts: Further Evidence", *Journal of Environmental Economics and Management*, Vol. 8, pp. 27-44.

Topfer, K. (1998), "Editorial comments on freshwater", *Our Planet*, Vol. 9, No. 4, pp. 3.

United Nations (1977), "Report of the United Nations Water Conference, Mar del Plata, 14-25 March, 1977", New York.

United Nations (1995), "World urbanization prospects: the 1994 revision: estimates and projections of urban and rural populations and of urban agglomerations", United Nations Dept. for Economic and Social Information and Policy Analysis Population Division, New York.

United Nations (2002), "Facts about Water. Fact Sheet, Johannesburg Summit 2002", Johannesburg, South Africa. Retrieved from: www.un.org/jsummit/html/media_info

United Nations Children's Fund (2003), "1.6m children die annually due to unclean water", The Punch, March 14, pp. 3.

United Nations (2006), "Millennium Development Goals report", United Nations Department of Economic and Social Affairs (DESA). www.un.org/millenniumgoals

WaterAid (2005), "National Water Sector Assessment, Ghana", pp. 2-4. http://www.wateraid.org/other/startdownload.asp?DocumentID=28&mode=plugin

Wattage, P. (2002), "Effective Management for Biodiversity Conservation in Sri Lankan Coastal Wetlands", Final Report A-I, Darwin Initiative, University of Portsmouth.

Wedgwood, A., and Sansom, K. (2003), *Willingness-to-pay surveys – A streamlined approach: Guidance notes for small town water services*. WEDC, Loughborough University, UK.

Whittington, D., Briscoe, J., Mu, X. and Barron, W. (1990), "Estimating the Willingness to Pay for Water Services in Developing Countries: A Case Study of the Use of Contingent Valuation Surveys in Southern Haiti", *Economic Development and Cultural Change*, Vol. 38, No. 2, pp. 293-311.

WHO and UNICEF (2000), "Global water supply and sanitation assessment 2000 report", World Health Organization, United Nations Children's Fund, Geneva, Switzerland, New York.

WHO and UNICEF (2004), "Joint Monitoring Programme for water supply and sanitation; meeting the MDG drinking water and sanitation target: A mid-term assessment of progress", WHO, Geneva.

Wood, S. and Trice, A. (1958) "Measurement of Recreation Benefits", *Land Economics*, Vol. 34, pp. 195-207.

Wooldridge J.M. (2002), *Econometric Analysis of Cross Section and Panel Data*, Massachusetts: MIT Press.

World Bank (1991), "Urban policy and economic development: an agenda for the 1990s", World Bank, Washington, D.C.

World Bank Water Demand Research Team (1993), "The Demand for Water in Rural Areas: Determinants and Policy Implications", *The World Bank Research Observer*, vol.8, No. 1, pp. 47-70.

World Health Organisation (1984), "Financial Management of Water Supply and Sanitation", A Hand Book.

World Health Organisation (2005), "Minimum water quantity needed for domestic use in emergencies", Technical Notes for Emergencies. Technical Note No. 9.

World Health Organisation (2006), "Country Health System Fact Sheet 2006, Ghana". http://www.afro.who.int/index.php?option=com_docman&task=doc_download&gid=37

Appendix A: Correlation Matrix for Explanatory Variables

```
. cor income Cost Time1 hseholdsize sex educ12 educ13 educ14 yearsstayed quality reliability initialbid inhouse maritalst
(obs=315)
```

	income	Cost	Time1	hsehol-e	sex	educ12	educ13	educ14	yearss-d	quality	reliab-y	initia-d	inhouse	marita-t
income	1.0000													
Cost	0.4126	1.0000												
Time1	0.3276	0.3536	1.0000											
hseholdsize	0.2763	0.4246	0.1948	1.0000										
sex	-0.3580	-0.0749	-0.0840	0.0063	1.0000									
educ12	-0.4008	-0.2973	-0.2953	-0.0825	0.2338	1.0000								
educ13	-0.1600	0.1166	0.0290	0.1261	0.0545	-0.4719	1.0000							
educ14	0.6499	0.2201	0.2471	-0.0404	-0.3379	-0.4415	-0.4546	1.0000						
yearsstayed	0.1340	0.3168	0.1659	0.3005	-0.0695	-0.1031	0.1250	0.0107	1.0000					
quality	-0.1486	-0.2191	-0.2098	-0.0680	-0.0776	0.1850	-0.0324	-0.1569	-0.0585	1.0000				
reliability	-0.1403	-0.3252	-0.3096	-0.1521	-0.0809	0.1404	-0.0387	-0.1144	-0.1172	0.4553	1.0000			
initialbid	-0.0740	-0.0412	-0.0046	-0.0388	0.1078	0.0820	-0.0740	-0.0375	-0.0620	0.0952	0.1228	1.0000		
inhouse	0.4088	0.2641	0.2620	0.0126	-0.1400	-0.3713	-0.0304	0.5013	0.0905	-0.1546	-0.0856	-0.0206	1.0000	
maritalst	0.1232	0.1715	0.2380	0.1201	-0.1043	-0.2098	0.0737	0.1535	0.1147	-0.1038	-0.1455	-0.0954	0.1568	1.0000

Appendix B: Test for Goodness of fit

Equivalent to R^2 in a conventional OLS regression model is the Likelihood Ratio Index (LRI) (also known as the pseudo R^2) which is used to test the goodness of fit for ordered probit model. LRI is computed by using the formula;

$$LRI = 1 - \frac{\ln L_{ur}}{\ln L_0}$$

Where lnL_{ur} is the log-likelihood value of the unrestricted function and lnL_0 is the log-likelihood value from a regression which has only the constant as the explanatory variable. The value of the LRI lies between "0" and "1".

If LRI=1, it implies that the model has a perfect fit. According Greene (2008), values between zero and one have no natural interpretation but as LRI approaches one it shows improvement in goodness of fit

The computed LRI value from our ordered probit model is given by;

$$LRI = 1 - \frac{-334.66194}{-495.56103}$$
$$= 0.3247$$

The computed ratio shows that the model seems adequate and it shows that it explains 32.47% of variations.

Appendix C: Econometric estimation of WTP for improved water supply system

```
. oprobit WTP income Cost Time1 hseholdsize sex educ12 educ13 educ14 yearsstayed quality reliability initialbid inhouse maritalst

Iteration 0:   log likelihood = -495.56103
Iteration 1:   log likelihood = -341.66639
Iteration 2:   log likelihood = -334.7214
Iteration 3:   log likelihood = -334.66197
Iteration 4:   log likelihood = -334.66194

Ordered probit regression                         Number of obs   =       315
                                                  LR chi2(14)     =    321.80
                                                  Prob > chi2     =    0.0000
Log likelihood = -334.66194                       Pseudo R2       =    0.3247
```

WTP	Coef.	Std. Err.	z	P>|z|	[95% Conf. Interval]	
income	.0007461	.0001241	6.01	0.000	.0005028	.0009893
Cost	.0014968	.0037444	0.40	0.689	-.005842	.0088356
Time1	.0066151	.0030266	2.19	0.029	.000683	.0125472
hseholdsize	-.021398	.0319181	-0.67	0.503	-.0839563	.0411602
sex	.2491386	.1404316	1.77	0.076	-.0261024	.5243795
educ12	.2494199	.2840308	0.88	0.380	-.3072702	.8061101
educ13	.5985087	.2889618	2.07	0.038	.0321539	1.164863
educ14	1.208878	.3408611	3.55	0.000	.5408029	1.876954
yearsstayed	.0111419	.0081091	1.37	0.169	-.0047516	.0270354
quality	-.4522656	.1789245	-2.53	0.011	-.8029512	-.10158
reliability	.1968602	.1609516	1.22	0.221	-.1185992	.5123196
initialbid	-1.727532	4.474383	-0.39	0.699	-10.49716	7.042098
inhouse	1.068704	.1622285	6.59	0.000	.7507422	1.386666
maritalst	.7582042	.1472494	5.15	0.000	.4696007	1.046808
/cut1	.7001755	.5627435			-.4027814	1.803132
/cut2	2.046886	.5680828			.9334643	3.160308
/cut3	3.339429	.5849957			2.192858	4.485999
/cut4	4.760365	.6131868			3.558541	5.962189

Appendix D: Estimated marginal effects of the Ordered Probit Model

```
. mfx, predict(outcome(1))

Marginal effects after oprobit
      y  = Pr(WTP==1) (predict, outcome(1))
         = .03083629
```

variable	dy/dx	Std. Err.	z	P>|z|	[95% C.I.]	x
income	-.0000519	.00001	-3.93	0.000	-.000078 -.000026	1001.17
Cost	-.0001042	.00026	-0.40	0.690	-.000616 .000408	41.1425
Time1	-.0004605	.00023	-2.01	0.044	-.000909 -.000012	38.7143
hsehol~e	.0014895	.00224	0.66	0.507	-.002906 .005885	5.14603
sex*	-.0175698	.01065	-1.65	0.099	-.038447 .003307	.514286
educ12*	-.0160152	.01715	-0.93	0.351	-.049637 .017607	.314286
educ13*	-.0356097	.01668	-2.13	0.033	-.068306 -.002914	.326984
educ14*	-.0624943	.01981	-3.15	0.002	-.101325 -.023664	.298413
yearss~d	-.0007756	.00058	-1.33	0.184	-.001921 .000369	8.78968
quality*	.0407764	.0213	1.91	0.056	-.000962 .082515	.203175
reliab~y*	-.0129053	.01028	-1.26	0.209	-.033045 .007235	.326984
initia~d	.1202531	.31173	0.39	0.700	-.490731 .731237	.097746
inhouse*	-.0687308	.01631	-4.21	0.000	-.100701 -.036761	.4
marita~t*	-.0714328	.02109	-3.39	0.001	-.112762 -.030103	.688889

(*) dy/dx is for discrete change of dummy variable from 0 to 1

```
. mfx, predict(outcome(2))

Marginal effects after oprobit
      y  = Pr(WTP==2) (predict, outcome(2))
         = .27002261
```

variable	dy/dx	Std. Err.	z	P>|z|	[95% C.I.]	x
income	-.0002078	.00004	-5.59	0.000	-.000281 -.000135	1001.17
Cost	-.0004169	.00104	-0.40	0.690	-.002463 .001629	41.1425
Time1	-.0018425	.00085	-2.16	0.031	-.003515 -.00017	38.7143
hsehol~e	.00596	.00889	0.67	0.502	-.01146 .02338	5.14603
sex*	-.0691624	.03914	-1.77	0.077	-.145867 .035169	.514286
educ12*	-.068505	.07671	-0.89	0.372	-.218849 .08184	.314286
educ13*	-.1589647	.07281	-2.18	0.029	-.30166 -.016269	.326984
educ14*	-.2881455	.06632	-4.34	0.000	-.418139 -.158152	.298413
yearss~d	-.0031034	.00227	-1.37	0.171	-.00755 .001343	8.78968
quality*	.1253848	.04896	2.56	0.010	.029418 .221352	.203175
reliab~y*	-.0543084	.04397	-1.24	0.217	-.140479 .031863	.326984
initia~d	.4811734	1.24755	0.39	0.700	-1.96397 2.92632	.097746
inhouse*	-.2712616	.04024	-6.74	0.000	-.350127 -.192396	.4
marita~t*	-.2044413	.04031	-5.07	0.000	-.283444 -.125439	.688889

(*) dy/dx is for discrete change of dummy variable from 0 to 1

```
. mfx, predict(outcome(3))

Marginal effects after oprobit
      y  = Pr(WTP==3) (predict, outcome(3))
         = .47867228
```

variable	dy/dx	Std. Err.	z	P>|z|	[95% C.I.]	x
income	.0000386	.00002	1.56	0.118	-9.8e-06 .000087	1001.17
Cost	.0000774	.0002	0.38	0.700	-.000317 .000471	41.1425
Time1	.0003419	.00027	1.29	0.199	-.000179 .000863	38.7143
hsehol~e	-.001106	.00175	-0.63	0.528	-.00454 .002328	5.14603
sex*	.0131529	.01123	1.17	0.242	-.008863 .035169	.514286
educ12*	.0080677	.00897	0.90	0.368	-.009515 .025651	.314286
educ13*	.0050087	.02078	0.24	0.810	-.035728 .045745	.326984
educ14*	-.0513037	.05109	-1.00	0.315	-.151446 .048839	.298413
yearss~d	.0005759	.00056	1.03	0.301	-.000515 .001667	8.78968
quality*	-.0465343	.03027	-1.54	0.124	-.105858 .012789	.203175
reliab~y*	.0073803	.00737	1.00	0.317	-.007062 .021822	.326984
initia~d	-.0892905	.24005	-0.37	0.710	-.559787 .381206	.097746
inhouse*	.0069076	.03164	0.22	0.827	-.0551 .068915	.4
marita~t*	.0774719	.03144	2.46	0.014	.01586 .139084	.688889

(*) dy/dx is for discrete change of dummy variable from 0 to 1

```
. mfx, predict(outcome(4))

Marginal effects after oprobit
      y  = Pr(WTP==4) (predict, outcome(4))
         = .20626271
```

variable	dy/dx	Std. Err.	z	P>|z|	[95% C.I.]		X
income	.0001942	.00004	5.03	0.000	.000118	.00027	1001.17
Cost	.0003896	.00097	0.40	0.689	-.00152	.0023	41.1425
Time1	.001722	.00081	2.13	0.033	.00014	.003305	38.7143
hsehol~e	-.0055703	.00836	-0.67	0.505	-.021956	.010816	5.14603
sex*	.0645575	.03647	1.77	0.077	-.006917	.136032	.514286
educ12*	.0663932	.07715	0.86	0.389	-.084812	.217599	.314286
educ13*	.1612249	.07866	2.05	0.040	.00705	.3154	.326984
educ14*	.3177252	.08192	3.88	0.000	.157164	.478287	.298413
yearss~d	.0029004	.00213	1.36	0.172	-.001265	.007066	8.78968
quality*	-.1071039	.03913	-2.74	0.006	-.183791	-.030417	.203175
reliab~y*	.0521268	.04369	1.19	0.233	-.033495	.137749	.326984
initia~d	-.4497044	1.16364	-0.39	0.699	-2.73039	1.83099	.097746
inhouse*	.2769619	.04542	6.10	0.000	.187947	.365977	.4
marita~t*	.1764748	.03414	5.17	0.000	.109568	.243382	.688889

(*) dy/dx is for discrete change of dummy variable from 0 to 1


```
. mfx, predict(outcome(5))

Marginal effects after oprobit
      y  = Pr(WTP==5) (predict, outcome(5))
         = .01420612
```

variable	dy/dx	Std. Err.	z	P>|z|	[95% C.I.]		X
income	.000027	.00001	2.92	0.003	8.9e-06	.000045	1001.17
Cost	.0000541	.00014	0.40	0.692	-.000213	.000321	41.1425
Time1	.0002391	.00013	1.84	0.066	-.000016	.000494	38.7143
hsehol~e	-.0007733	.00117	-0.66	0.510	-.003075	.001528	5.14603
sex*	.0090218	.00584	1.54	0.122	-.002426	.02047	.514286
educ12*	.0100592	.01311	0.77	0.443	-.015628	.035746	.314286
educ13*	.0283408	.01952	1.45	0.147	-.009921	.066602	.326984
educ14*	.0842183	.0433	1.95	0.052	-.000646	.169083	.298413
yearss~d	.0004027	.00032	1.27	0.205	-.000221	.001026	8.78968
quality*	-.012523	.00556	-2.25	0.024	-.023418	-.001628	.203175
reliab~y*	.0077065	.00712	1.08	0.279	-.006257	.02167	.326984
initia~d	-.0624316	.16284	-0.38	0.701	-.381595	.256732	.097746
inhouse*	.0561228	.01816	3.09	0.002	.020524	.091722	.4
marita~t*	.0219274	.00786	2.79	0.005	.006524	.037331	.688889

(*) dy/dx is for discrete change of dummy variable from 0 to 1

Appendix E: Estimation of the Demand Equation

The Household Demand schedule is given by;

Pesewas per Bucket (Y)	Number of Households (X)
18.05	109,330
14.05	271,271
10.05	466,915
6.05	697,084
2.00	822,033

The Demand equation is estimated by regressing X on Y. The result is shown below;

```
. regress y x

    Source |       SS       df       MS              Number of obs =       5
-----------+------------------------------           F(  1,    3) =  423.83
     Model | 159.671794     1   159.671794           Prob > F      =  0.0003
  Residual | 1.1301935      3   .376731168           R-squared     =  0.9930
-----------+------------------------------           Adj R-squared =  0.9906
     Total | 160.801988     4   40.2004969           Root MSE      =  .61378

         y |      Coef.   Std. Err.      t    P>|t|     [95% Conf. Interval]
         x |  -.0000215   1.04e-06   -20.59   0.000    -.0000248   -.0000182
     _cons |    20.2224    .5656612   35.75   0.000     18.42221    22.02258
```

Therefore the Equation of the Household Demand curve is given by;

$$Y = 20.2224 - 0.0000215X$$

This implies that,

$$X = 940576.7442 - 46511.62791Y$$

In finding the corresponding X values for Y=5 (half of the mean WTP) and Y=10 (the mean WTP), we have

Pesewas per Bucket (Y)	Number of Households (X)
5	708,018.6047
10	475,460.4651

From the tabulation of the open ended WTP elicitation question, we found out that both the mode, median and mean WTP equals **GH¢0.10** per bucket.

```
. sum wtp1

    Variable |      Obs        Mean    Std. Dev.       Min        Max
-------------+--------------------------------------------------------
        wtp1 |      315    .1000635    .0545129        .02         .2


. tab wtp1

        wtp1 |      Freq.     Percent        Cum.
-------------+-----------------------------------
         .02 |         16        5.08        5.08
        .025 |          5        1.59        6.67
         .03 |         12        3.81       10.48
        .035 |          2        0.63       11.11
         .04 |         13        4.13       15.24
         .05 |         47       14.92       30.16
        .055 |          2        0.63       30.79
         .06 |         21        6.67       37.46
        .065 |          1        0.32       37.78
         .07 |          9        2.86       40.63
        .075 |          1        0.32       40.95
         .08 |          7        2.22       43.17
         .09 |          4        1.27       44.44
        .095 |          1        0.32       44.76
          .1 |         54       17.14       61.90
         .11 |          1        0.32       62.22
         .12 |         15        4.76       66.98
         .13 |          1        0.32       67.30
         .14 |          9        2.86       70.16
         .15 |         50       15.87       86.03
         .16 |          2        0.63       86.67
         .17 |          2        0.63       87.30
         .18 |         12        3.81       91.11
          .2 |         28        8.89      100.00
-------------+-----------------------------------
       Total |        315      100.00
```

Appendix F: Estimation of Various Consumer Surpluses and Expected Total Revenue Using different tariff levels (Current tariff level of GHp1.45, half of the mean WTP which equals GHp5 and the mean WTP of GHp10).

(i) Improving the water supply system, charging the current tariff level with supply left unconstrained.

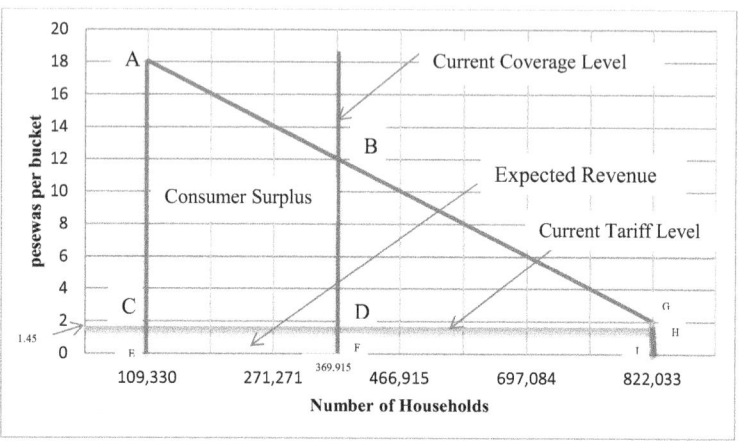

Figure A.1: Expected revenue and consumers' surplus from charging the current tariff.

The possible consumer surplus and expected total revenue that would be derived from improving the water supply system, charging the current price of GHp1.45 per bucket with supply left unconstrained is given by the areas of trapezoid CHGA and rectangle EIHC respectively. The areas of trapezoid CHGA and rectangle EIHC represent the possible consumer surplus and total revenue that would accrue to households and service providers if each household consumer one bucket of water. Therefore to calculate the consumer surplus and expected total revenue per day, the areas of the trapezoid and the rectangle should be multiplied by the average household consumption of water (20.4 buckets) per day.

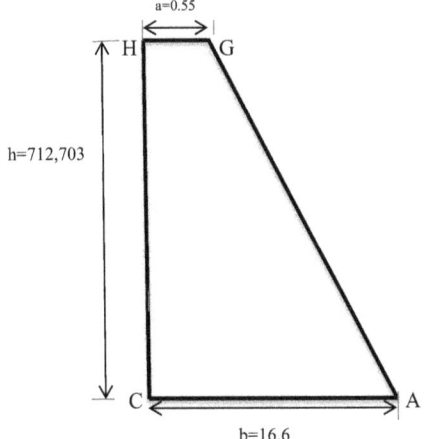

Area of trapezoid (CAGH) = $\frac{1}{2}$ * height * [a + b]

$\quad\quad\quad\quad\quad\quad\quad\quad\quad\; =\; \frac{1}{2}(712{,}703)[0.55 + 16.6]$

$\quad\quad\quad\quad\quad\quad\quad\quad\quad\; =\; 0.5 * 712{,}703 * 17.15$

$\quad\quad\quad\quad\quad\quad\quad\quad\quad\; =\; 6{,}111{,}428.225$

Therefore the possible consumer surplus (GHp6,111,428.225*20.4) that would be accrued to households is GHp124,673,135.8 which is equal to GH¢1,246,731.35 per day.

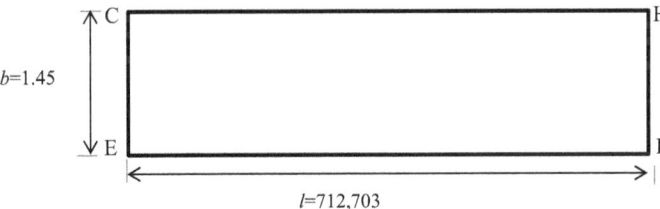

Area of rectangle (EIHC) = $length(l) * breadth(b)$

$\quad\quad\quad\quad\quad\quad\quad\quad\quad\;\; =\; 712{,}703 * 1.45$

$\quad\quad\quad\quad\quad\quad\quad\quad\quad\;\; =\; 1{,}033{,}419.35$

Therefore the expected total revenue (GHp1,033,419.35*20.4) that would be accrued to the service provider is GHp21,081,754.74 which is equal to GH¢210,817.54 per day.

(ii) Improving the water supply system, charging the current tariff level with constrained supply as a result of supply constraints (insufficient funds and infrastructure).

Due to supply constraints (insufficient funds and infrastructure) only 369,915 households representing 45% of the total number of households in the metropolis would be covered and thus the consumer surplus and expected total revenue that would accrue to households and the service provider if each household consume one bucket of water are represented by the areas of trapezoid CABD and rectangle EFDC respectively.

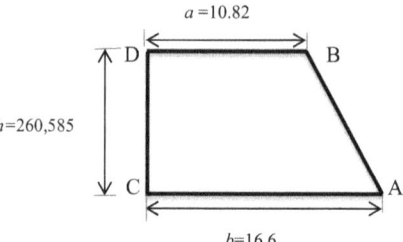

Area of trapezoid (CABD) = $\frac{1}{2}$ * height * [a + b]

= $\frac{1}{2}$(260,585)[10.82 + 16.6]

= 0.5 * 260,585 * 27.42

= 3,572,620.35

Therefore the possible consumer surplus (which is calculated by multiplying the average household water consumption of 20.4 buckets by the area of the trapezoid CABD) that would be accrued to households is GH¢728,814.55 per day.

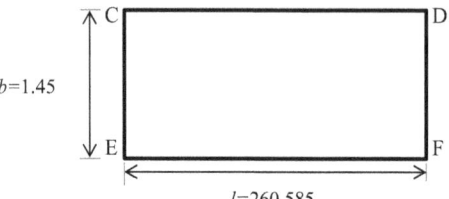

Area of rectangle (EFDC) = $length(l) * breadth(b)$

= 260,585 * 1.45

= 377,848.25

Therefore the expected total revenue (which is calculated by multiplying the average household water consumption of 20.4 buckets by the area of rectangle EFDC) that would be accrued to the service provider is GH¢77,081.04 per day.

(iii) Improving the water supply system and charging GHp5 (half of mean WTP) with supply being assured.

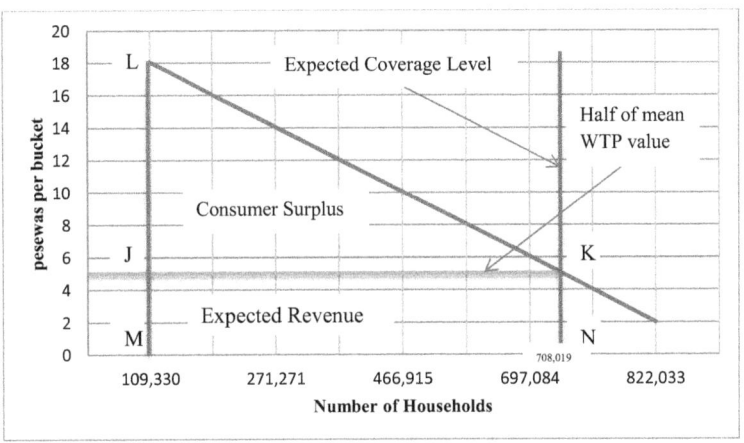

Figure A.2: Expected Revenue and consumers' surplus from charging half of the mean WTP.

The possible consumer surplus and expected total revenue that would accrue to households and the service provider if each household consume one bucket of water are represented by the areas of triangle JKL and rectangle MNKJ respectively.

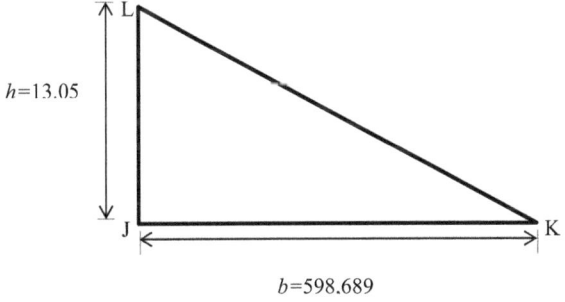

$$\text{Area of triangle (JKL)} = \frac{1}{2} * base(b) * height(h)$$
$$= 0.5 * 598{,}689 * 13.05$$
$$= 3{,}906{,}445.725$$

Therefore the possible consumer surplus (which is calculated by multiplying the average household water consumption of 20.4 buckets by the area of the triangle JKL) that would be accrued to households is GH¢796,914.93 per day.

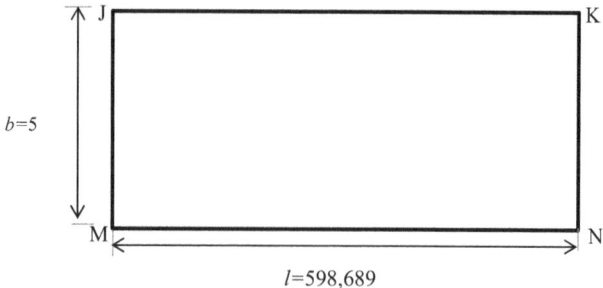

Area of rectangle (MNKJ) = $length(l) * breadth(b)$
= $598,689 * 5$
= $2,993,445.00$

Therefore the expected total revenue (which is calculated by multiplying the average household water consumption of 20.4 buckets by the area of the rectangle MNKJ) that would be accrued to the service provider is GH¢610,662.78 per day.

(iv) Improving the water supply system and charging GHp10 (mean WTP) with supply being assured.

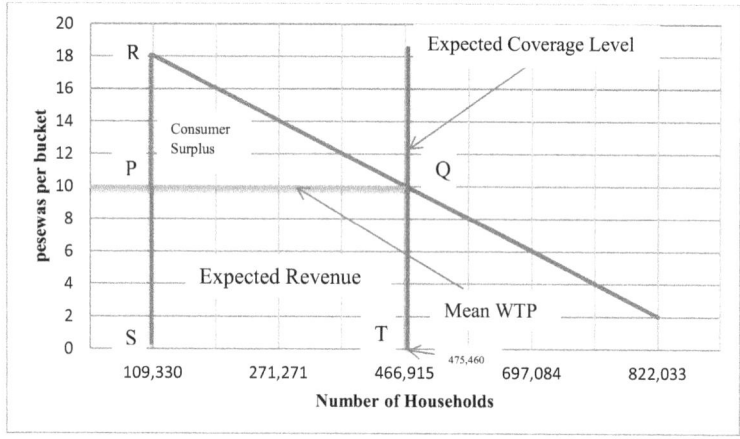

Figure A.3: Expected Revenue and consumers' surplus from charging the mean WTP.

The possible consumer surplus and expected total revenue that would accrue to households and the service provider if each household consume one bucket of water are represented by the areas of triangle PQR and rectangle STQP respectively.

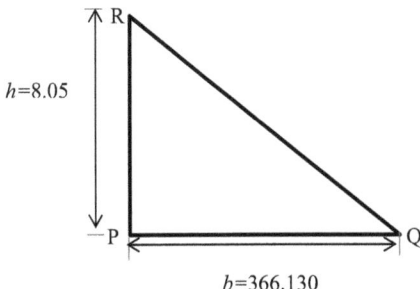

Area of triangle (PQR) = $\frac{1}{2} * base(b) * height(h)$
= $0.5 * 366{,}130 * 8.05$
= $1{,}473{,}673.25$

Therefore the possible consumer surplus (which is calculated by multiplying the average household water consumption of 20.4 buckets by the area of the triangle PQR) that would be accrued to households is GH¢300,629.34 per day.

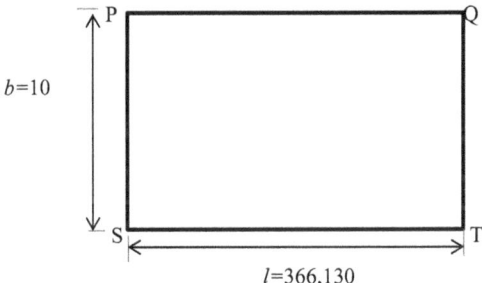

Area of rectangle (STQP) = $length(l) * breadth(b)$
= $366{,}130 * 10$
= $3{,}661{,}300.00$

Therefore the expected total revenue (which is calculated by multiplying the average household water consumption of 20.4 buckets by the area of the rectangle STQP) that would be accrued to the service provider is GH¢746,905.20 per day.

Appendix G: Contingent Valuation Survey Questionnaire

Code [ ]   Enumeration Area [ ]

Interviewer_____

Place of Interview: _____

Date of interview_____

> **UPPERCASE LETTERS REFER TO INSTRUCTIONS FOR INTERVIEWERS**
>
> **Lower case letters refer to questions and information to be read to the interviewee.**

INTRODUCTION

Hello, I am_____, a research enumerator from the University of Ghana assisting in data collection for an ongoing research by Mr. Ebo Botchway in partial fulfilment for the award of Master of Philosophy Degree in Economics. We are interviewing a sample of households in the Accra-Tema metropolis with the aim of estimating the WTP for improved water supply in the Accra-Tema metropolis. Please be assured that information provided would not in any way be linked to you and would be treated with utmost confidentiality. This interview is completely confidential and strictly for academic purposes and therefore honest discussion is the best way ahead.

SECTION A: EXISTING WATER USE CONDITIONS AND PROBLEMS

A1. What is the main source of water for the members of this household?

   1. Private piped water   2. Shared piped water in compound   3. Public tap/Stand pipes
   4. Tanker Operators   5. Boreholes   6. Well   7. Other (Specify) _____

> IF "IN-HOUSE PIPED WATER" (1 and 2) ASK A2, A3, A4, A5, A6, A7 and A8

A2. How many days in a week do water flow? _____

A3. How many hours in a day do water flow? _____

A4. How much do you pay a month? _____ Ghana cedis _____ pesewas

A5. What is your alternative source of water if there is no water running through the pipes?

   1. Public tap/Stand pipes 2. Tanker Operators 3. Boreholes 4. Well 5. Other (Specify) __

A6. How much money do you spend on this source in a day? __ Ghana cedis ___ pesewas

A7. How much do you pay per bucket from this source? _____ pesewas

A8. How much time do you spend to collect water from this source? __ Hours ___ Minutes

> **IF NOT "IN-HOUSE PIPED WATER" (1 and 2) ASK A9, A10, A11 and A12.**

A9. Why do you prefer this source if not <u>Piped water</u> system (Private or Shared)?

   1. No Access to Existing piped water system 2. I cannot afford the cost of Piped water system

   3. This source is Reliable   4. Lower volume charge 5. Other (Specify) __

A10. How much time do you spend to collect water from source? _____ Minutes

A11. Approximately how much money do you spend on water a day? _Ghana cedis__ pesewas

A12. How much do you pay per bucket from this source? _____ pesewas

> **ASK ALL RESPONDENTS THE FOLLOWING QUESTIONS (A13, A14 and A15)**

A13. To what extent do you perceive the current provision of <u>Piped water</u>, an issue worth discussing?

   1. Very Serious   2. Serious   3. Not Serious

A14. In relation to its <u>Quality</u>, <u>Quantity</u>, and <u>Reliability</u>, how do you rank the current status of water service from this source?

   1. QUALITY: 1. Excellent   2. Very Good   3. Good   4. Poor   5. Very Poor

   2. QUANTITY: 1. Excellent   2. Very Good   3. Good   4. Poor   5. Very Poor

   3. RELIABILITY: 1. Excellent 2. Very Reliable 3. Reliable 4. Moderately Reliable

              5. Unreliable

A15. In your opinion, has the administrative body done enough to solve the problem of providing <u>Piped water</u> to households?

   1. Yes   2. No

SECTION B: THE EXISTING SANITATION PRACTICE

B1. What type of Sanitation (Toilet facility) system does this household use?

   1. In house Facility: a). Flush toilet   b). Pit latrine   c). Other (Specify) _____

   2. No Facility in house: a). Public latrine b). Bush   c). Streets   d). Other (Specify) __

B2. If not **In house facility**, how far is this system from your house?

   1. Very Long   2. Long   3. Short   4. Very Short

B3. If **public latrine**, how much do your household spend on this facility in a day?

   ___ Ghana cedis _____ Ghana pesewas

B4. How satisfied are you with the use of this system?

    1. Very Satisfied   2. Satisfied   3. Not satisfied

SECTION C: WILLINGNESS TO PAY QUESTIONS
HYPOTHETICAL SCENARIO

In the next section of the questionnaire, I would like to ask you how much it is worth to you in monetary terms, the provision of improved water service. The provision of improved water service among other things means, good quality water which is safe for all household purposes including drinking, available at every time. Also the family need not spend its time and effort in fetching water from distant sources.

Let us assume that you have an option for a private connection to such an improved piped water supply scheme. Also assume that you will be charged a monthly water fee based on the volume of water your household consume in a month. You may not be required to pay initially for the costs of connection to the new scheme. The payment will be built-in the monthly water bill and paid over several years.

ASK THE WTP QUESTIONS

C1. Do you think your household would be willing to pay **GHp**_____ per bucket for the service?
    1. Yes   **Go to C2**
    2. No   **Go to C3**

IF YES INCREASE THE BID BY GHp 2.0   IF NO REDUCE THE BID BY GHp 2.0

C2. We do not know how much the GWCL will charge for this service in a month. If the decision is for the household to pay a rate of **GHp** _____ per bucket would your household be willing to pay for the service?
    1. Yes   **Go to C4**
    2. No   **Go to C6**

C3. We do not know how much the GWCL will charge for this service in a month. If the decision is for the household to pay a rate of **GHp** _____ per bucket would your household be willing to pay for the service?
    1. Yes   **Go to C6**
    2. No   **Go to C5**

C4. Would your household be willing to pay **GHp** _____ per bucket for this service?
    1. Yes   **Go to C6**
    2. No   **Go to C6**

C5. Would your household be willing to pay **GHp** _____ per bucket for this service?
    1. Yes   **Go to C6**
    2. No   **Go to C6**

C6. Think for a moment, what is the largest amount of money your household would be willing to pay per bucket to use this service? If it would cost your household more than this amount, your household could not afford to pay and would not be able to use the service.
    Amount of money_____ Ghana pesewas per bucket

SECTION D: SOCIO-ECONOMIC CHARACTERISTICS

D1. Sex: 1. Male   2. Female

D2. Age: 1. 0-29 years   2. 30-39 years   3. 40-49 years   4. 50-59 years   5. Above 60

D3. Marital Status: 1. Married   2. Otherwise

D4. Education Level: 1. No Education   2. Basic   3. Secondary   4. Tertiary

D5. What is your main Occupation? _____

D6. How long have you been staying in this house? _____ Years

D7. How long do you plan to stay in this house/area? _____ Years

D8. How many individuals are in this household? _____ individuals

D9. How many of them are working? _____ individuals

D10. What is the total income of this household?(Sum of income of all who are working) GH¢ __

D11. Please list the following in order of importance to the household (List for instance, first, second, third, etc.).

    1. School _____   2. Health _____   3. Electricity _____

    4. Water _____   5. Sanitation _____   6. Road _____

D12. How would you rank the proposed improved water services in the future?

    1. Excellent   2. Very Good   3. Good   4. Poor   5. Very Poor

THANK YOU.

Appendix H: How Sachet water producers stores their raw material (water) using water produced by the GWCL.

Figure A4: Polytanks containing water to be used for sachet water production.

Appendix I: An example of burst pipe resulting in UfW

Figure A5: A picture of a pipe spilling over.

i want morebooks!

Buy your books fast and straightforward online - at one of world's fastest growing online book stores! Environmentally sound due to Print-on-Demand technologies.

Buy your books online at
www.get-morebooks.com

Kaufen Sie Ihre Bücher schnell und unkompliziert online – auf einer der am schnellsten wachsenden Buchhandelsplattformen weltweit! Dank Print-On-Demand umwelt- und ressourcenschonend produziert.

Bücher schneller online kaufen
www.morebooks.de

VDM Verlagsservicegesellschaft mbH
Heinrich-Böcking-Str. 6-8   Telefon: +49 681 3720 174   info@vdm-vsg.de
D - 66121 Saarbrücken   Telefax: +49 681 3720 1749   www.vdm-vsg.de

Lightning Source UK Ltd.
Milton Keynes UK
UKHW011006150421
382040UK00001B/126